hotel
seventeen

Special Thanks to:

My Parents

Prof. Jürgen Heinemann
Uli Braunagel und Tobias Zeller
Nick Waplington
Janson Farrla
Codie
Sigrid Haugen
Neal Schofield
Justin Desmond Meltale
Mike Kirk
Jeffrey
Tamara Schlesinger
Michaele Laudig
Michael Reetz
Amanda Lepore
Ryan Williams
Desire
Ingrid de Granier
Daniel Müller
Shevis Clem
Francoise Steibel
Bettina Schmitt
Marcus Wasserberg
Miranda Darling
Marcelo Krasilcic
Jean-Marc
Manuel Alcalá Albarán
Luke und Danny Copeland
Windscale
Miriam Schell und Alfred Nrecaj
Jennifer Pellegrin
Kiren Chang
Thomas Schwarz
Achim Liebsch
Marion Beckhäuser
Bill Candis – Hotel Seventeen
Flatiron Color Lab Inc. New York
Thomas Meyer – Performing Light Inc. New York
HENSEL Studiotechnik
Kodak Professional
Hasselblad
Insa Müller
Gabi Maibaum

Susanne Bornemann

First published in the UK by
Dewi Lewis Publishing
8 Broomfield Road
Heaton Moor
Stockport SK4 4ND
+44 (0)161 442 9450
Web Site: www.dewilewispublishing.com

ISBN: 1-899235-03-5

Design by Jörg Fokuhl and Dewi Lewis
Printed in Germany by Wachter, Bönnigheim

Jörg Fokuhl

hotel seventeen

DEWI LEWIS
PUBLISHING

to Franziska

Hotel Seventeen on Manhattan´s 17th Street is one of the more affordable hotel alternatives in New York City. It offers the basics, and cheaply – room only, no breakfast, shared facilities – it is hardly luxury. On the front desk a receptionist maintains round the clock security via eye contact, as the extraordinary array of guests come and go.

Yet, this Hotel celebrates a special tradition. Here, you will come across visionaries – or perhaps they are just dreamers. People who have travelled from all over the world to the culture capital of New York, full of optimism and great expectations – young actors, fashion designers, photographers, models, film college students, punk and rock musicians, drag queens.

Stars like Madonna, David Bowie or Woody Allen have been spotted at Hotel Seventeen, as they arrive for a quick photo-shoot or perhaps a movie scene. Inspired by such fleeting moments of glamour, yet with only a hazy notion of their own goals, many of the hotel guests continue to live the dream that their talent will be discovered. And as they wait, supporting themselves through a variety of part-time jobs, Hotel Seventeen often becomes their 'home' not just for the weeks they had expected, but for months and, for some, even years.

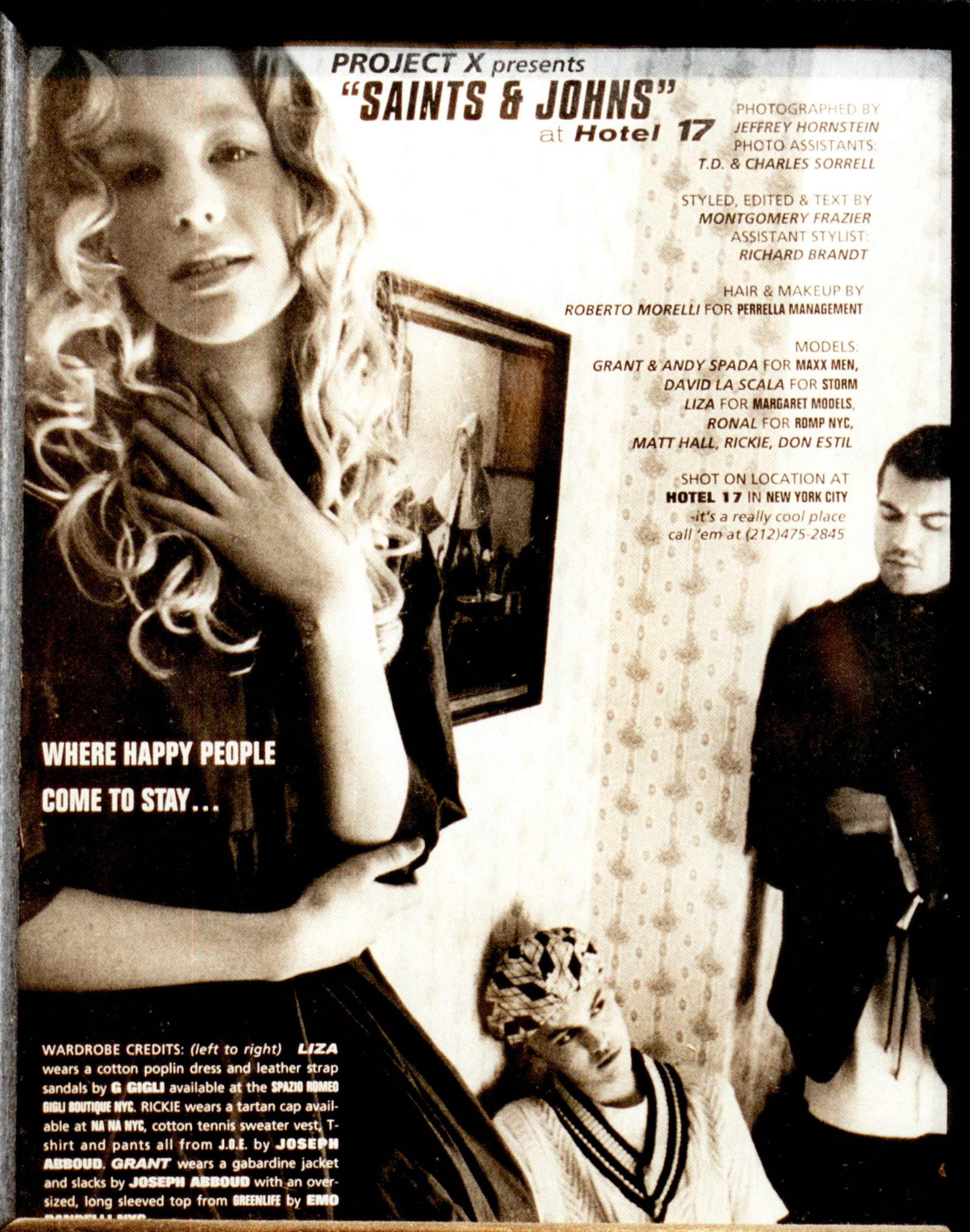
PROJECT X presents
"SAINTS & JOHNS"
at Hotel 17
PHOTOGRAPHED BY JEFFREY HORNSTEIN
PHOTO ASSISTANTS: T.D. & CHARLES SORRELL
STYLED, EDITED & TEXT BY MONTGOMERY FRAZIER
ASSISTANT STYLIST: RICHARD BRANDT
HAIR & MAKEUP BY ROBERTO MORELLI FOR PERRELLA MANAGEMENT
MODELS: GRANT & ANDY SPADA FOR MAXX MEN, DAVID LA SCALA FOR STORM LIZA FOR MARGARET MODELS, RONAL FOR ROMP NYC, MATT HALL, RICKIE, DON ESTIL
SHOT ON LOCATION AT HOTEL 17 IN NEW YORK CITY -it's a really cool place call 'em at (212)475-2845
WHERE HAPPY PEOPLE COME TO STAY...
WARDROBE CREDITS: (left to right) LIZA wears a cotton poplin dress and leather strap sandals by G GIGLI available at the SPAZIO ROMEO GIGLI BOUTIQUE NYC. RICKIE wears a tartan cap available at NA NA NYC, cotton tennis sweater vest, T-shirt and pants all from J.O.E. by JOSEPH ABBOUD. GRANT wears a gabardine jacket and slacks by JOSEPH ABBOUD with an oversized, long sleeved top from GREENLIFE by EMO

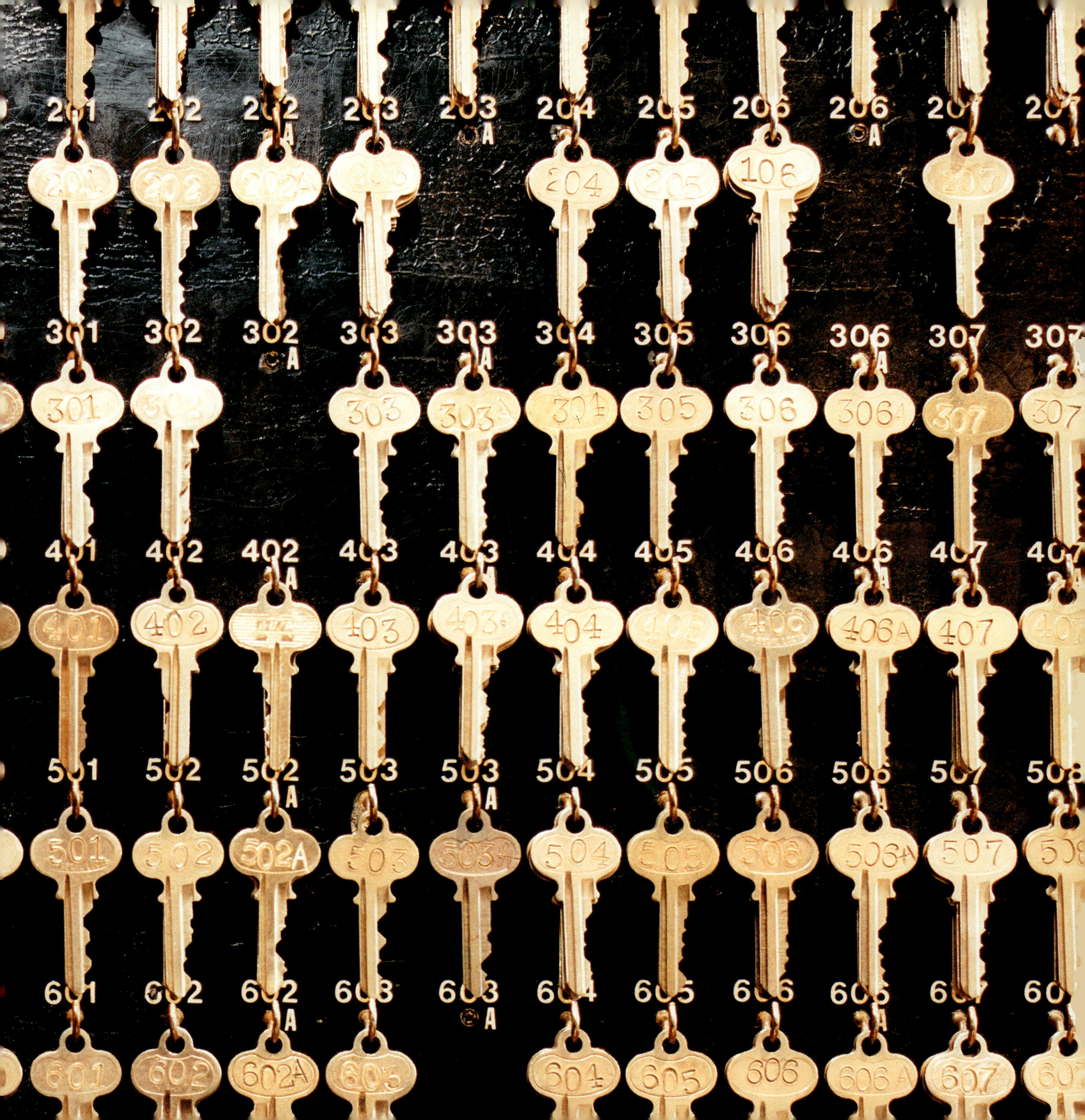

204
205
106
301
303
303A
305
306
306A
402
403
404
406A
407
501
502
502A
503
504
507
601
602
602A
604
605
606

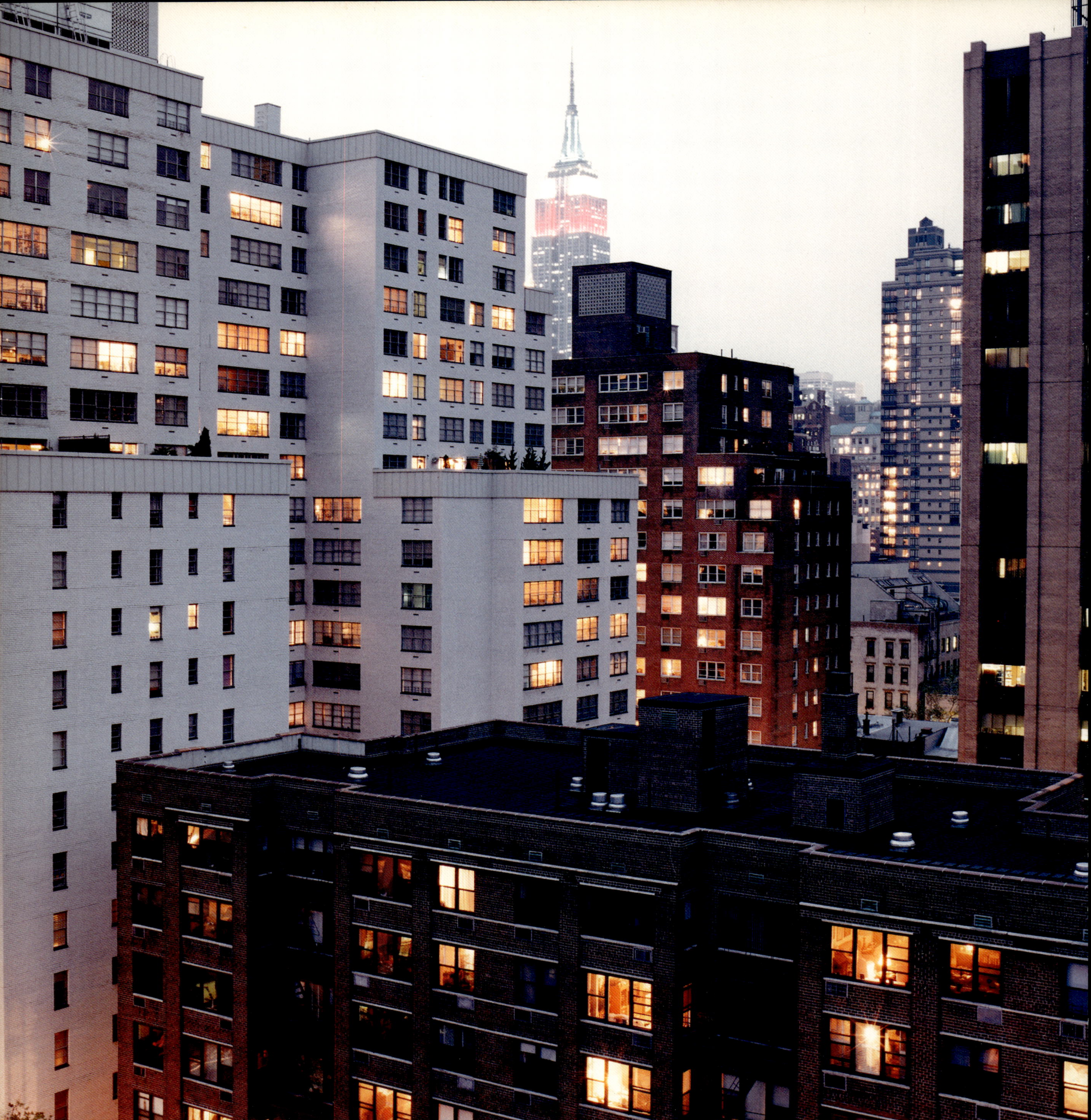

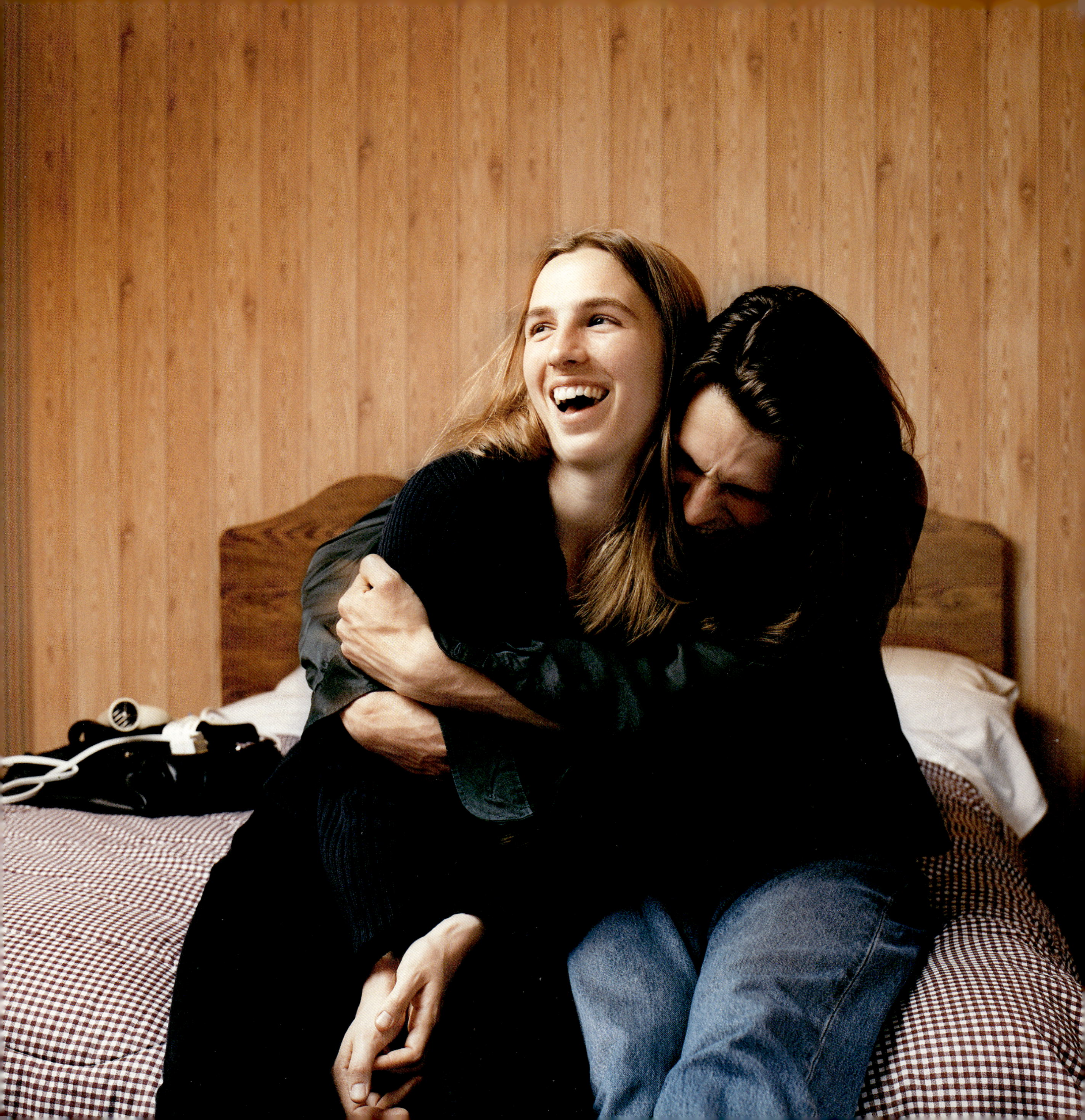

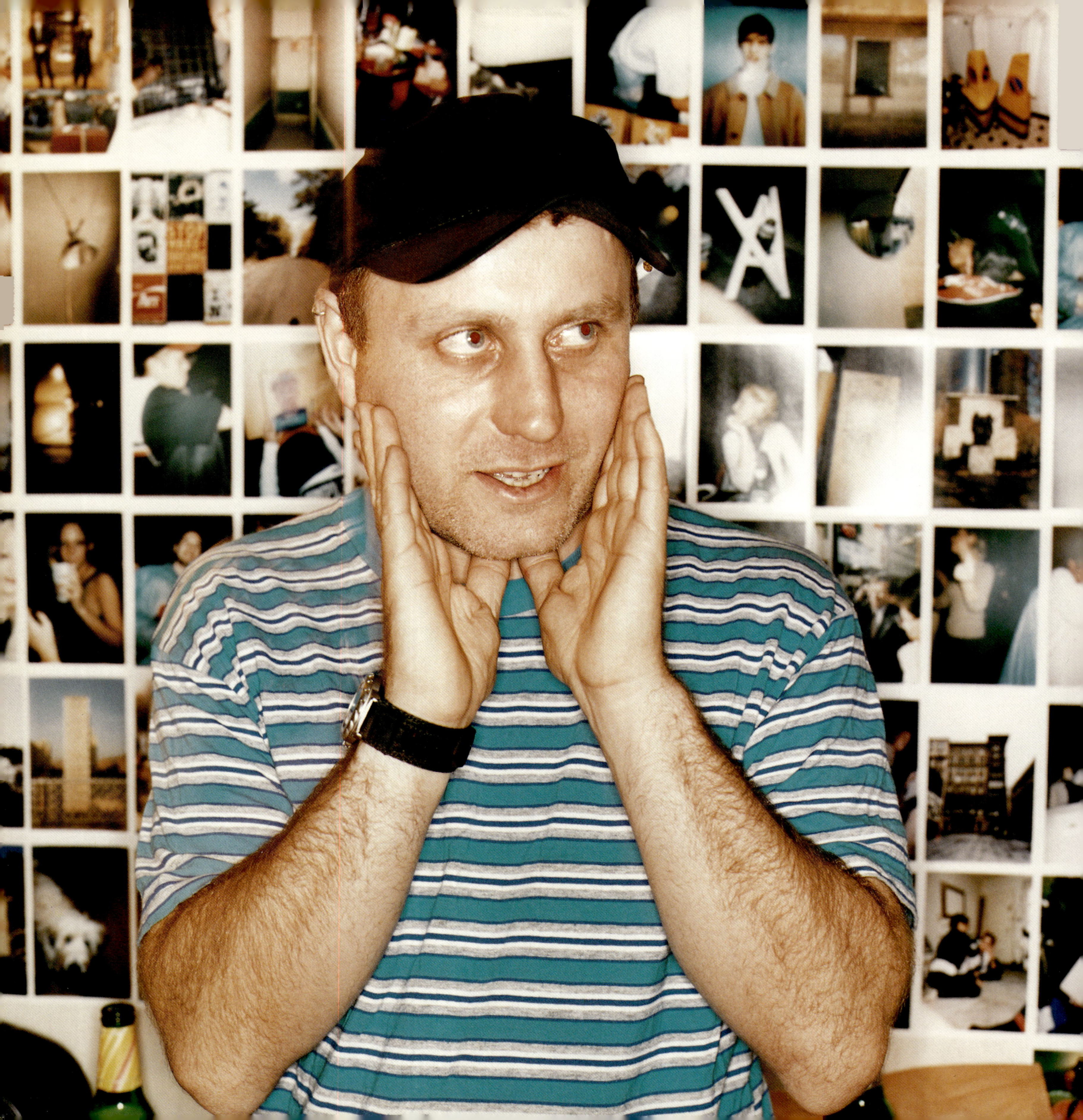

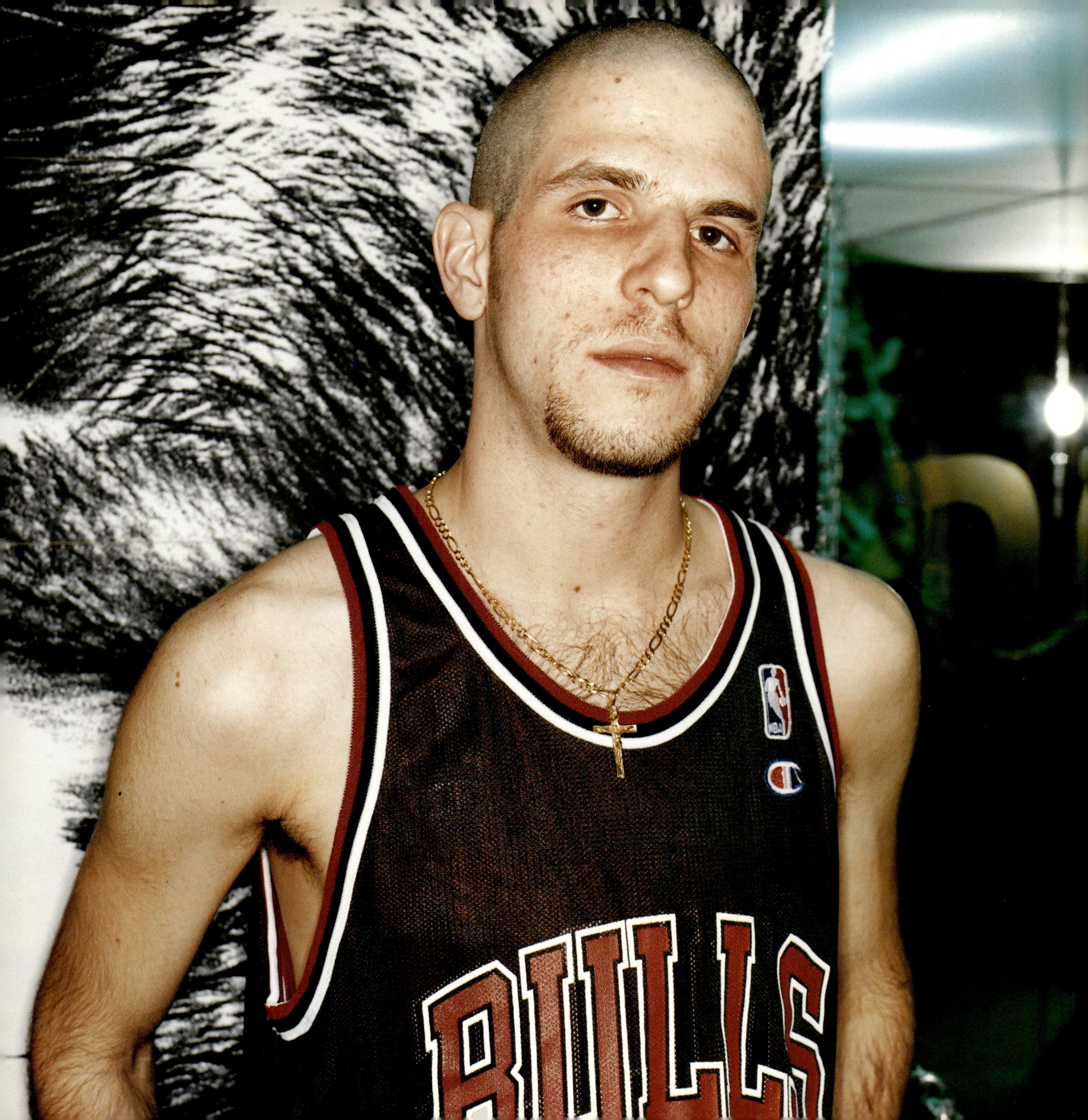
BULLS

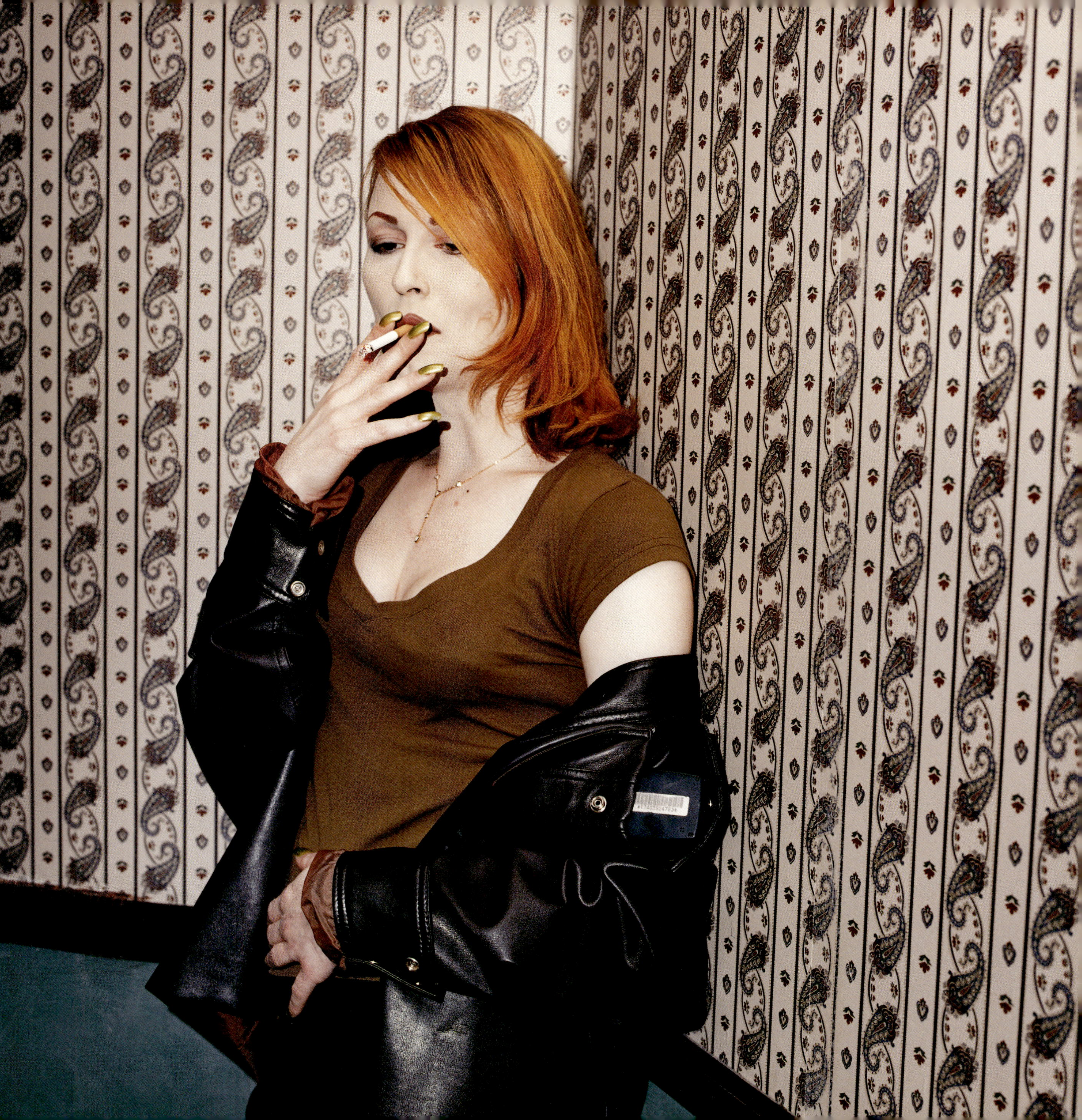

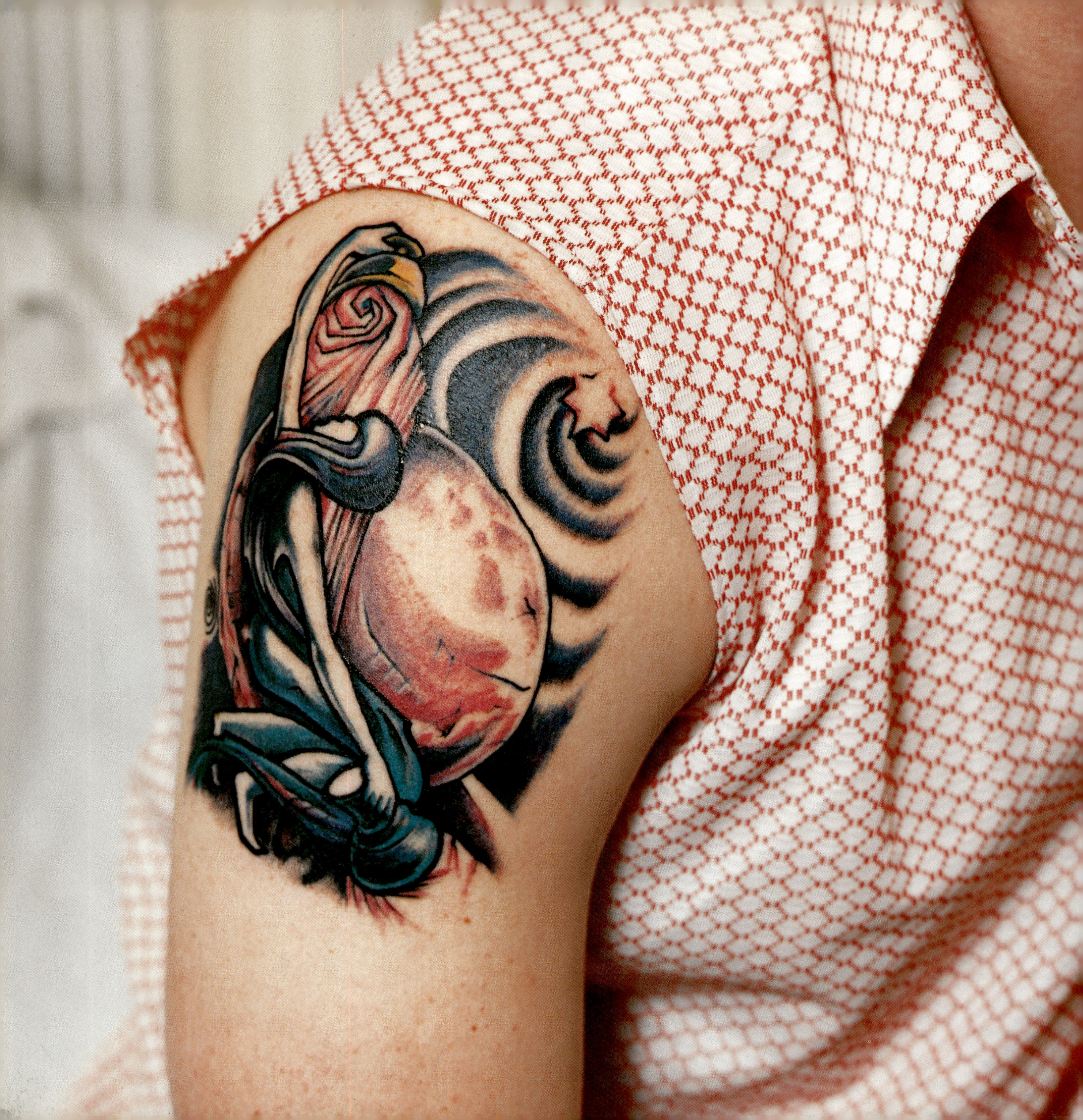

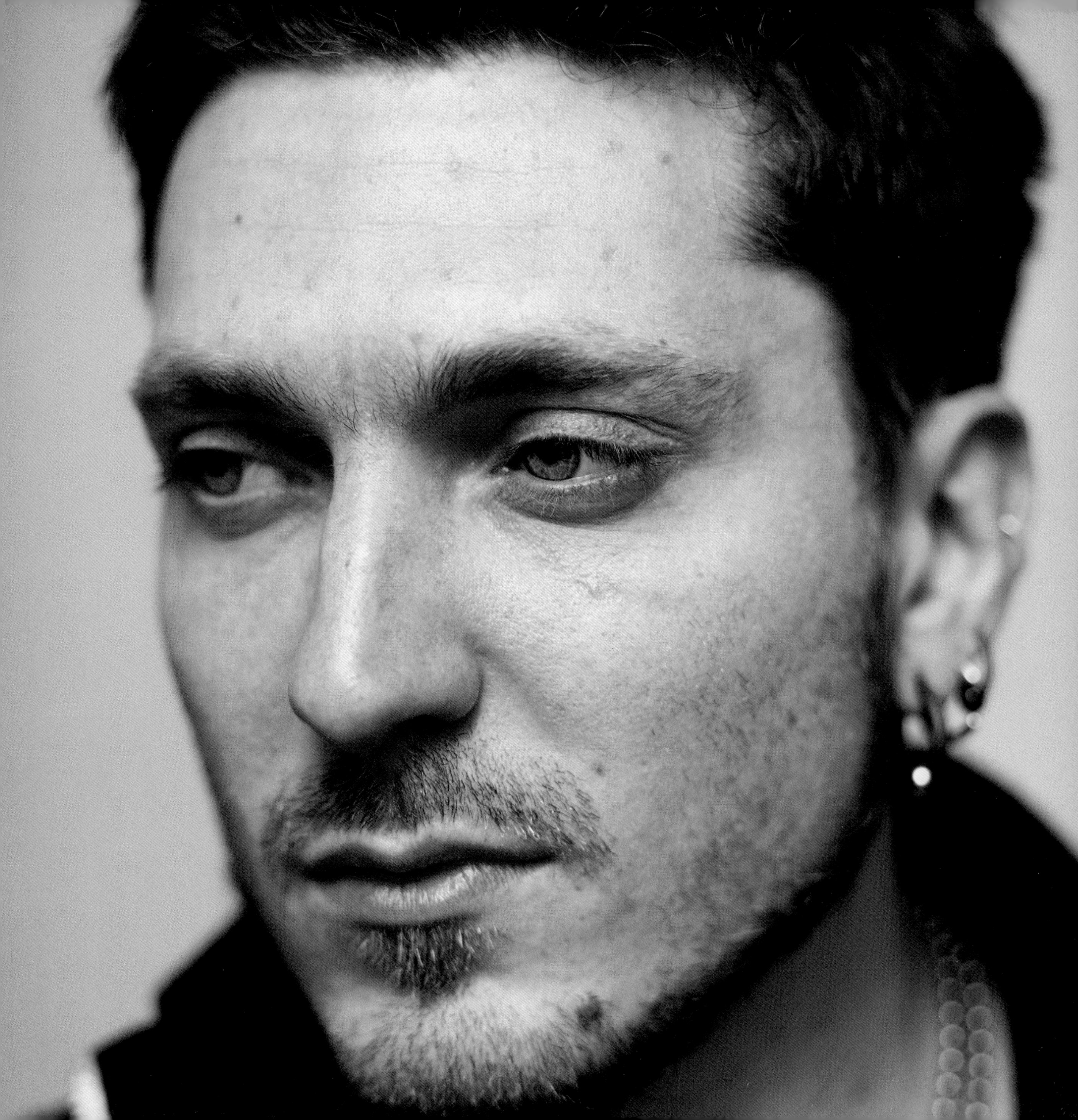

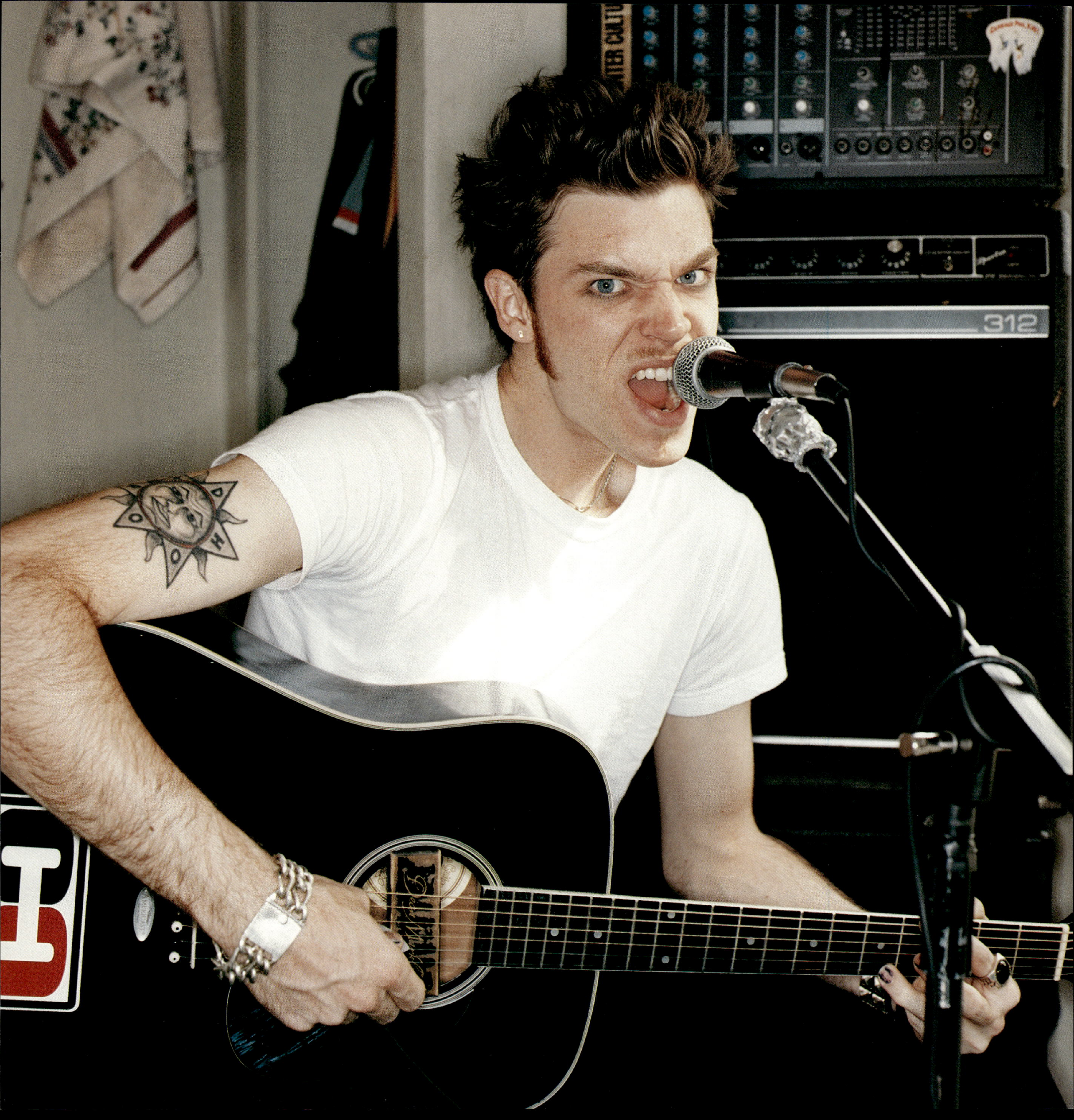
312

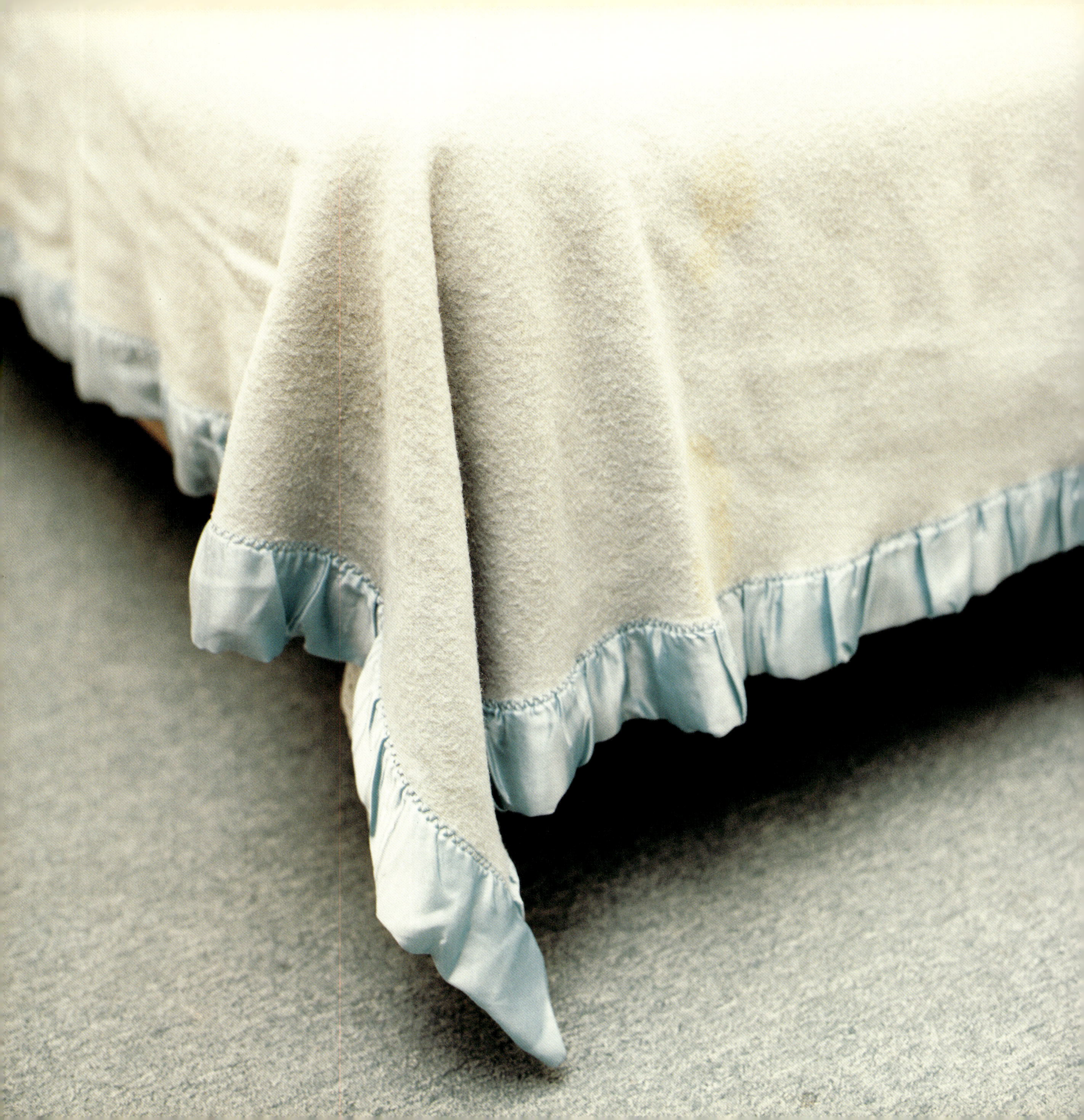

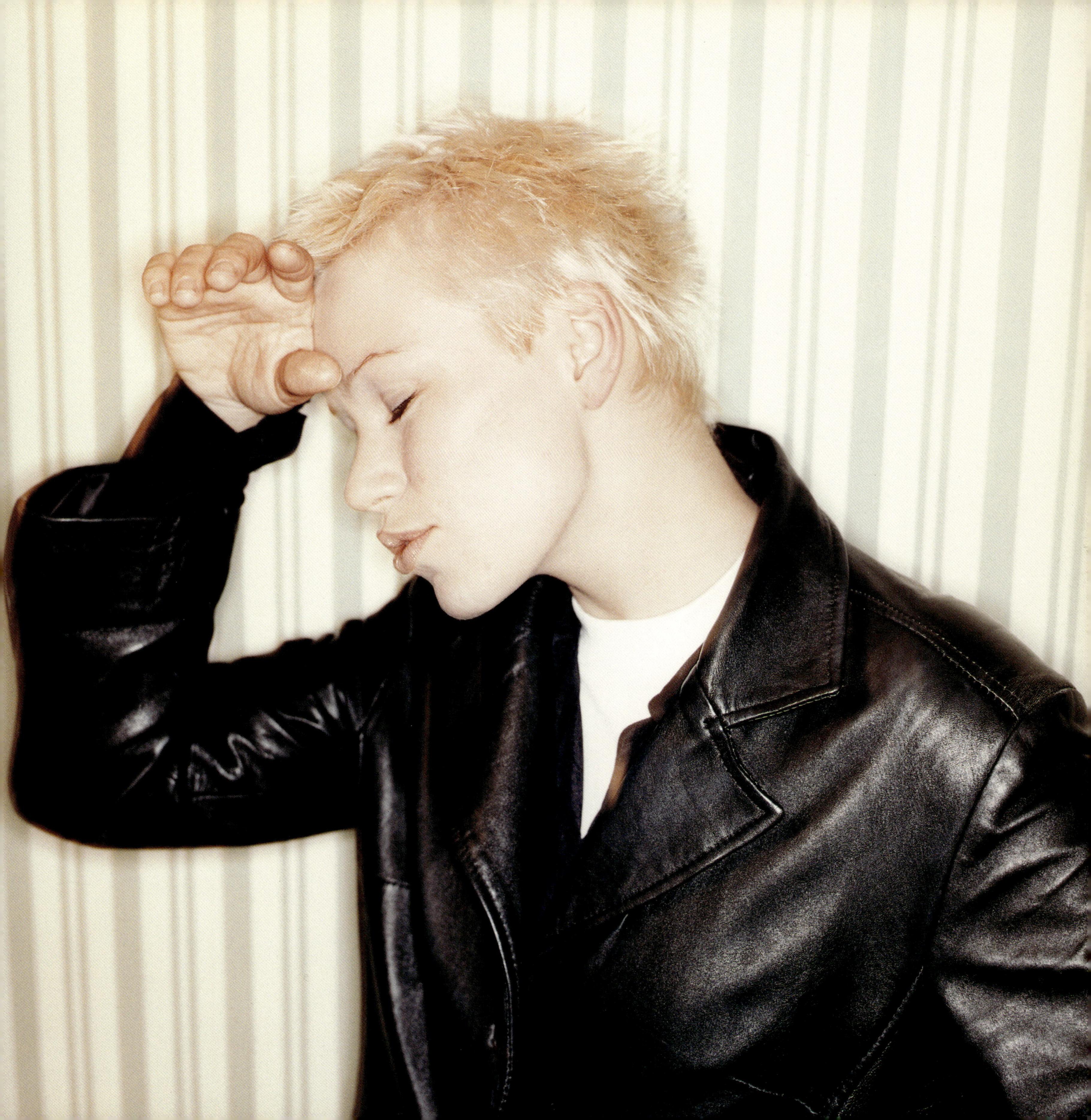

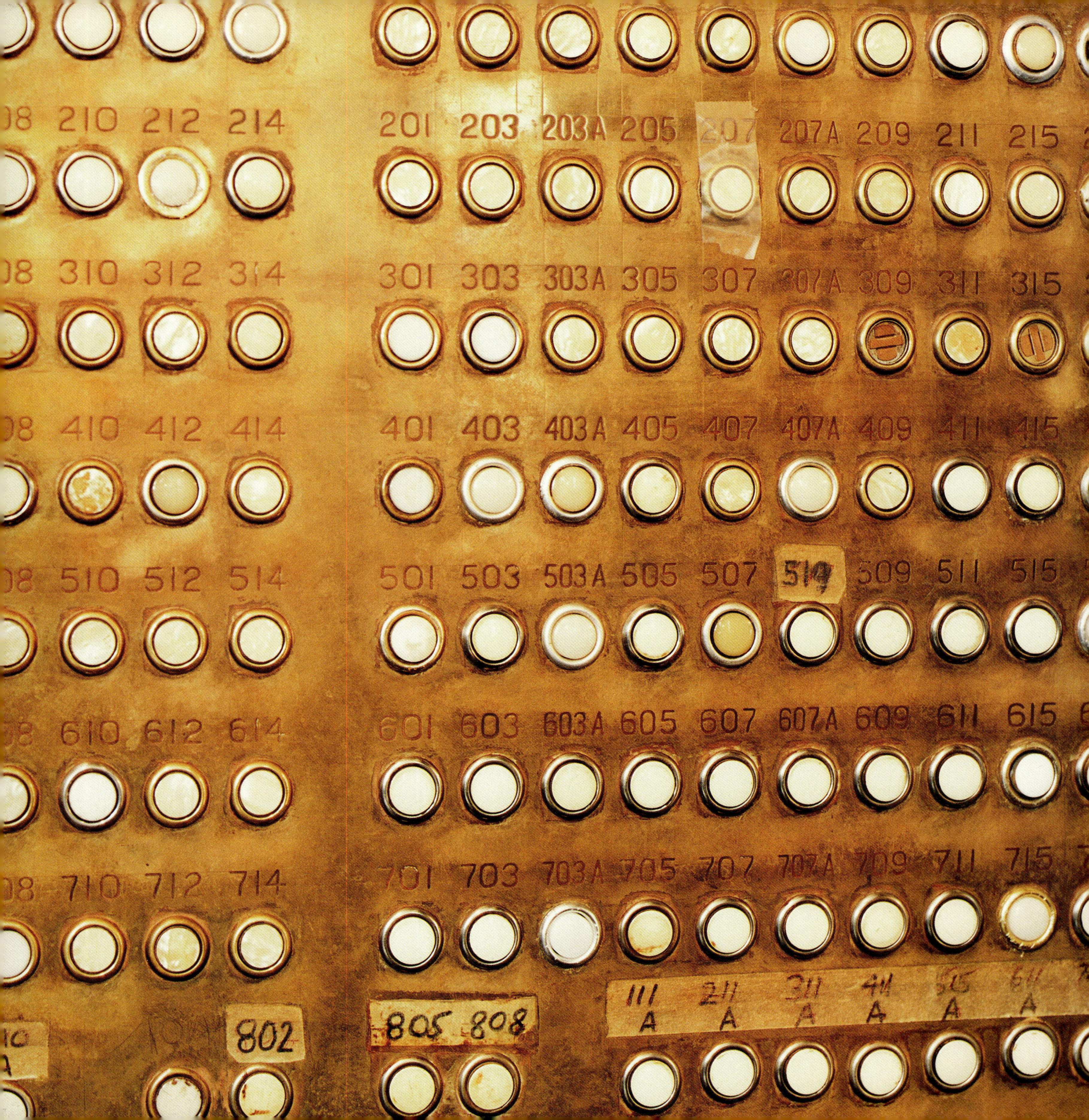
210 212 214 201 203 203A 205 207 207A 209 211 215
310 312 314 301 303 303A 305 307 307A 309 311 315
410 412 414 401 403 403A 405 407 407A 409 411 415
510 512 514 501 503 503A 505 507 519 509 511 515
610 612 614 601 603 603A 605 607 607A 609 611 615
710 712 714 701 703 703A 705 707 707A 709 711 715
802
805 808
111 A 211 A 311 A 411 A 611 A

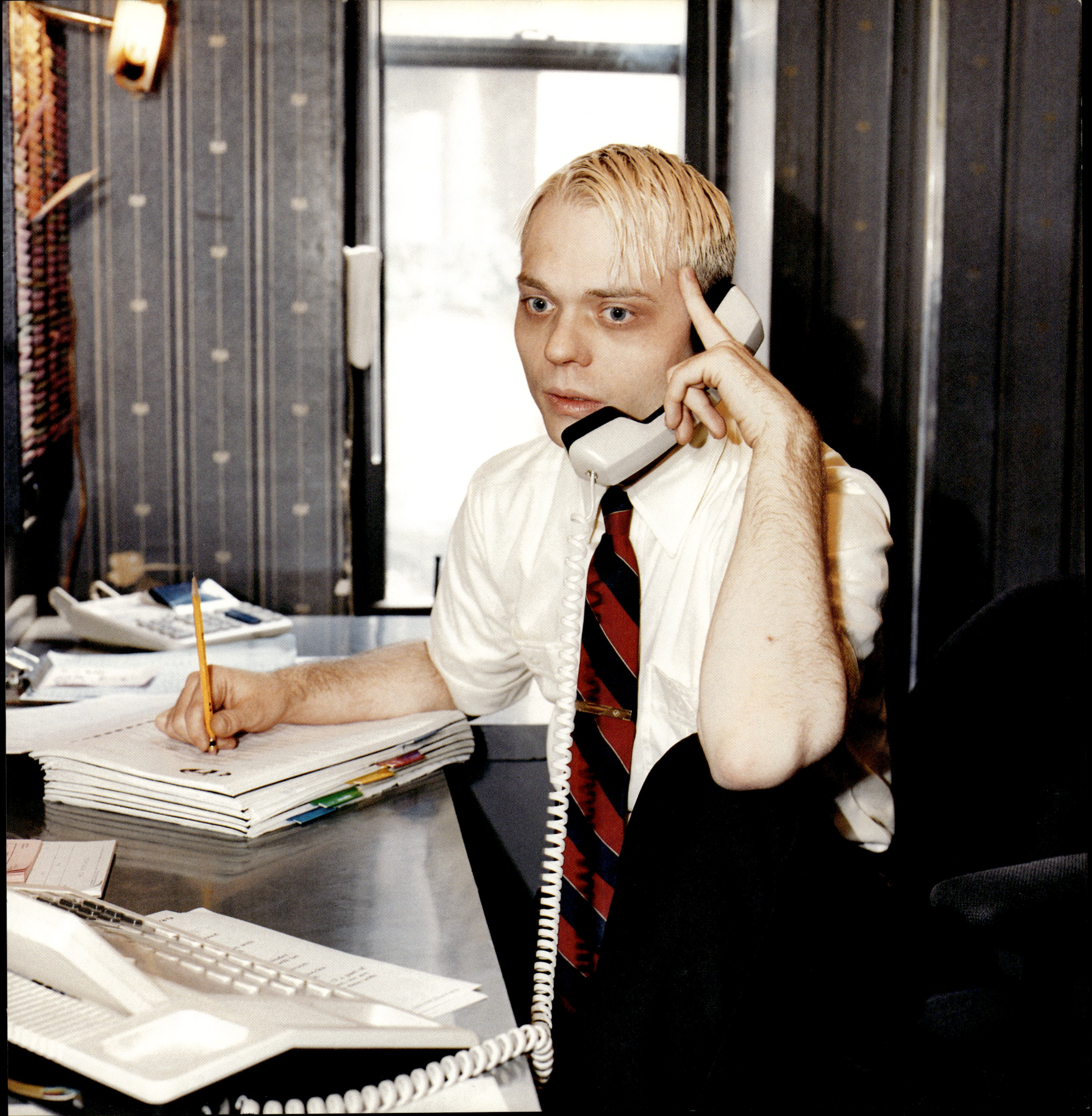

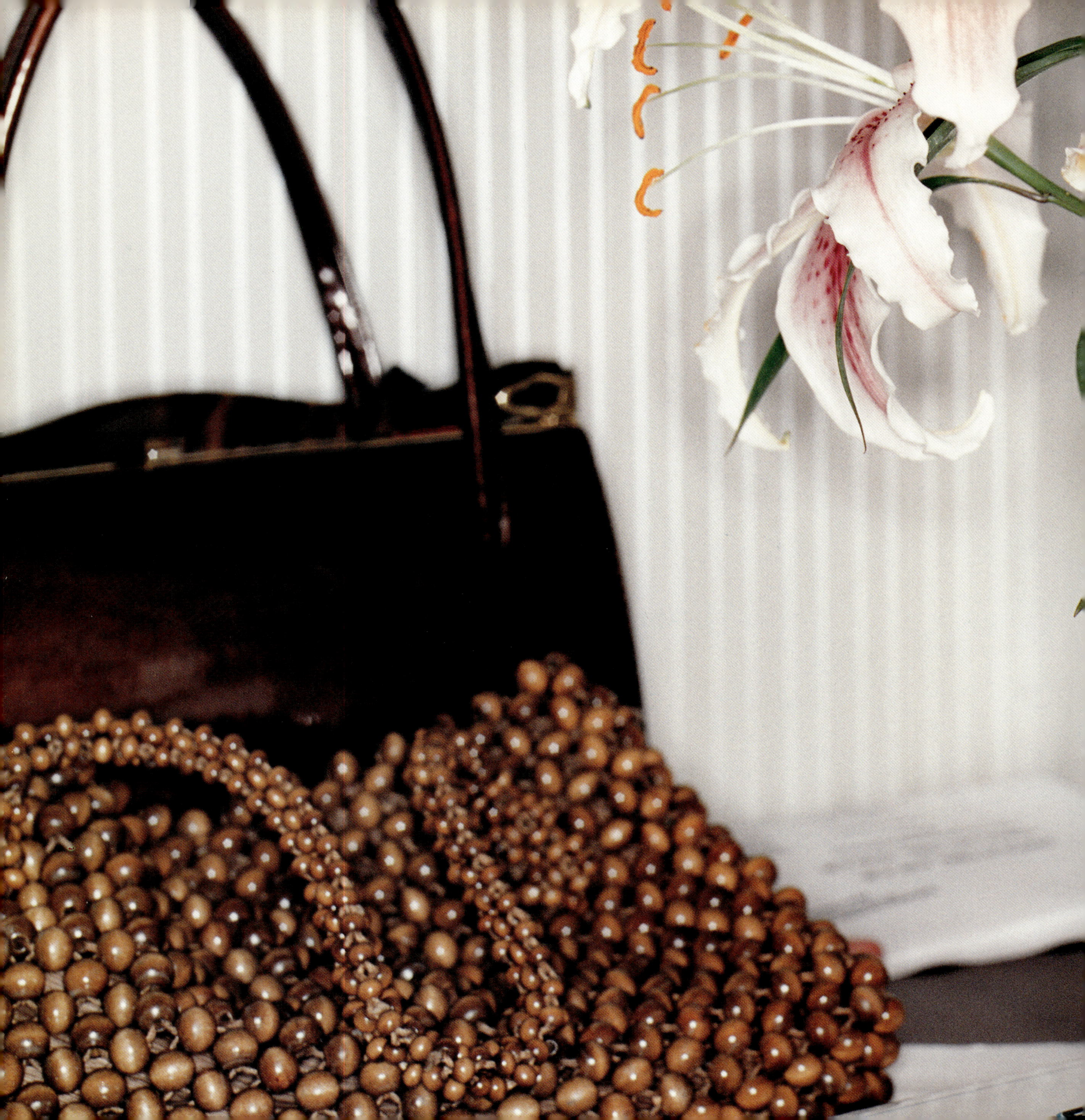

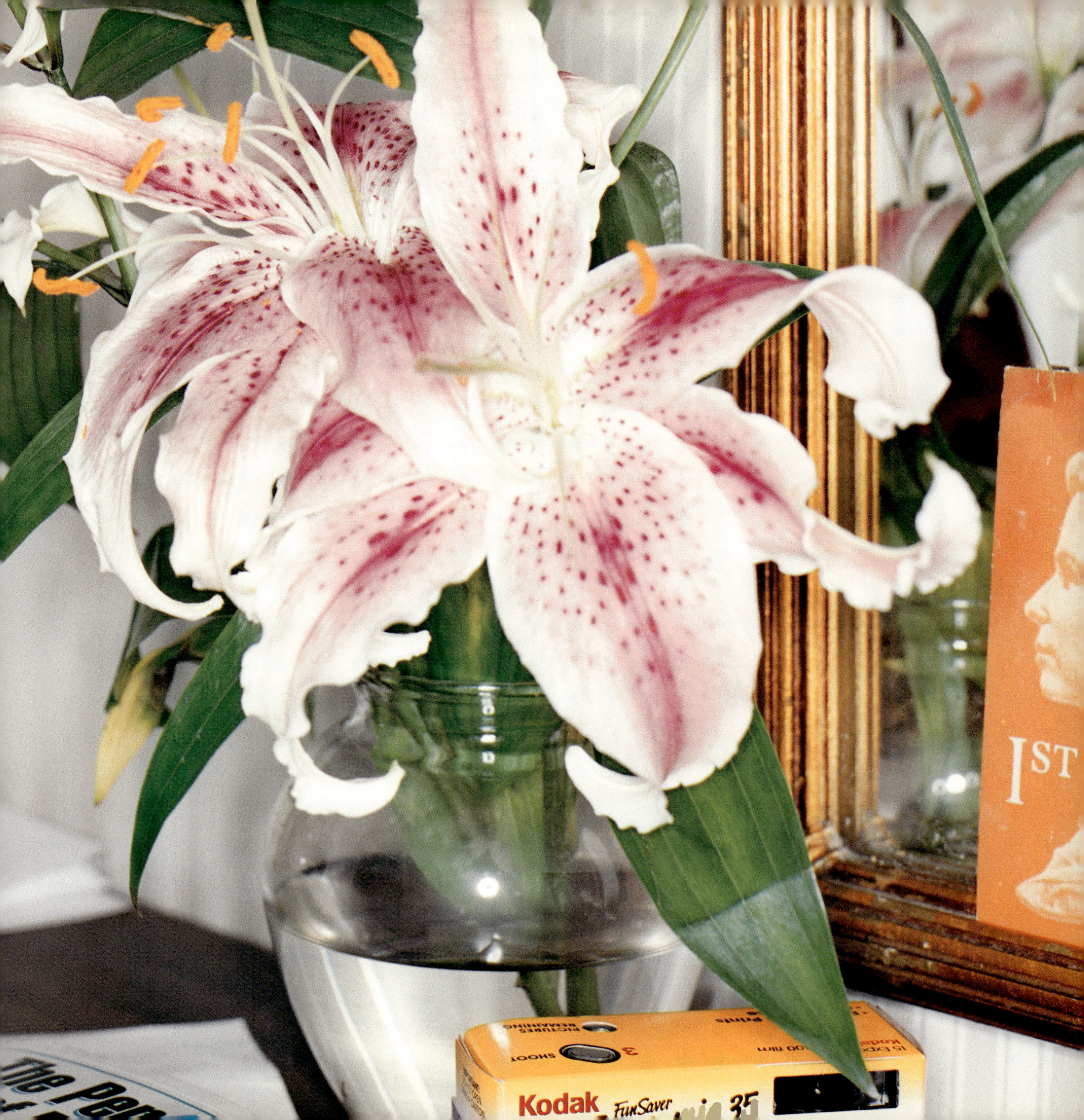
1ST
Kodak
FunSaver

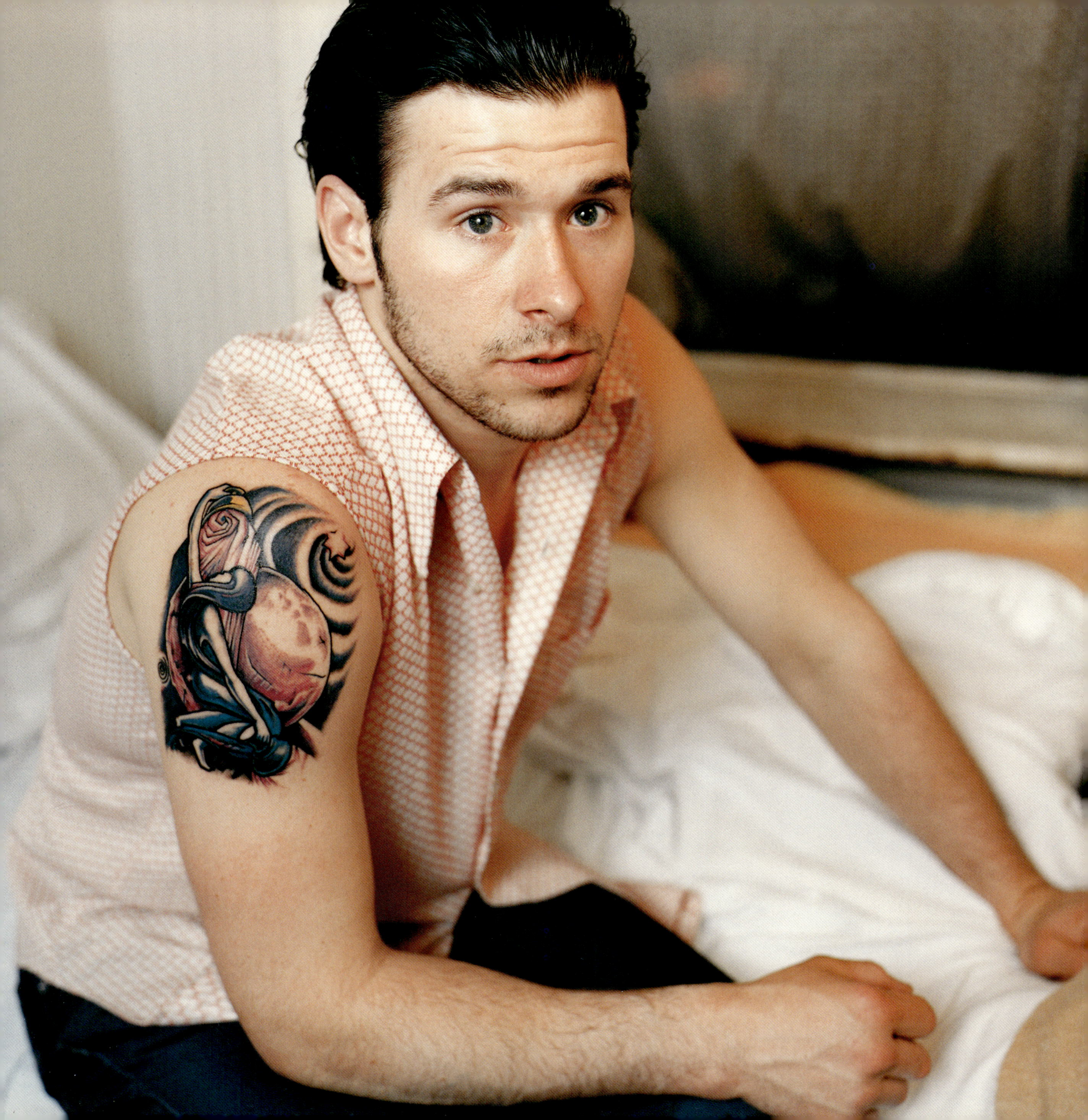

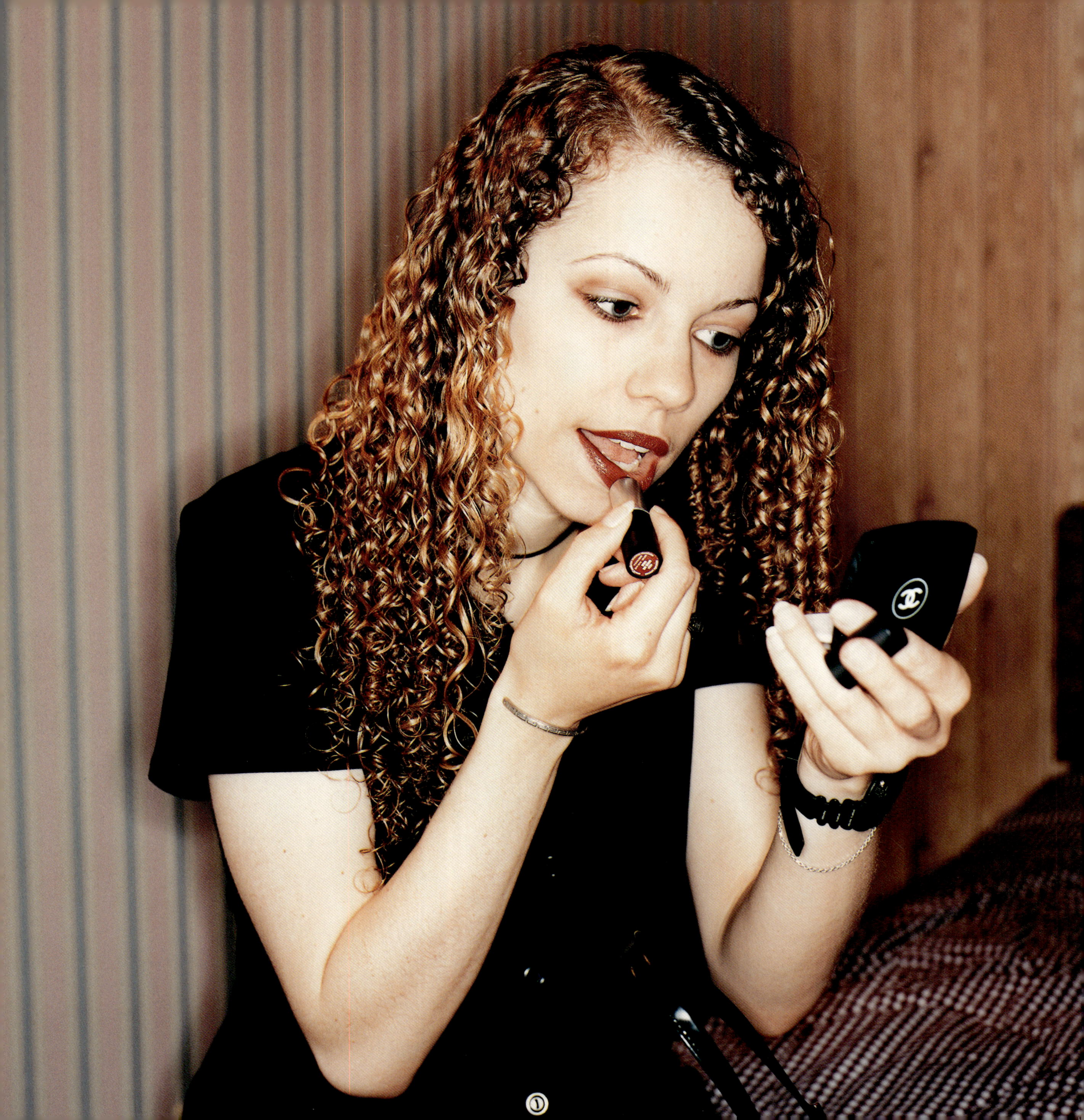

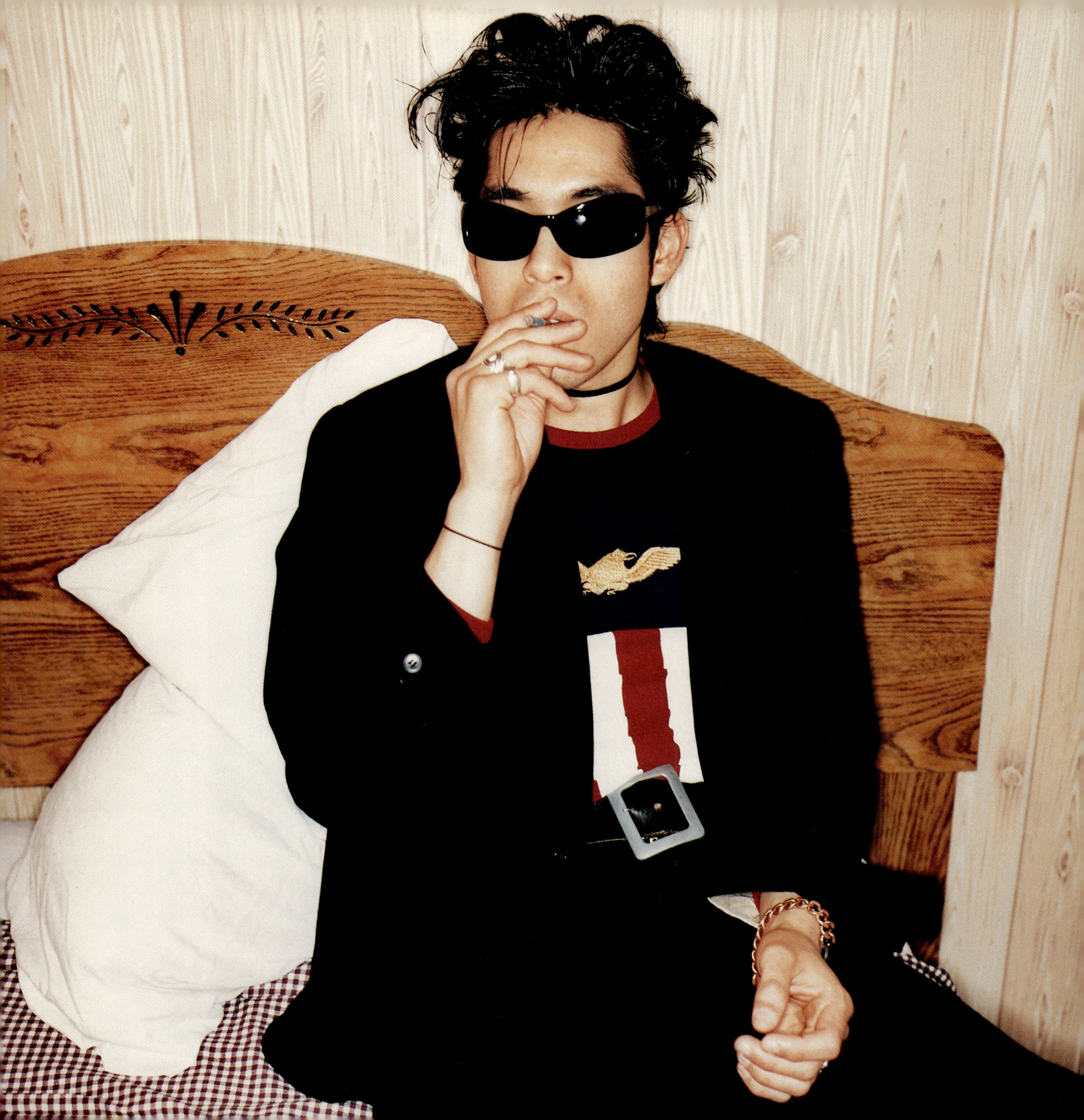

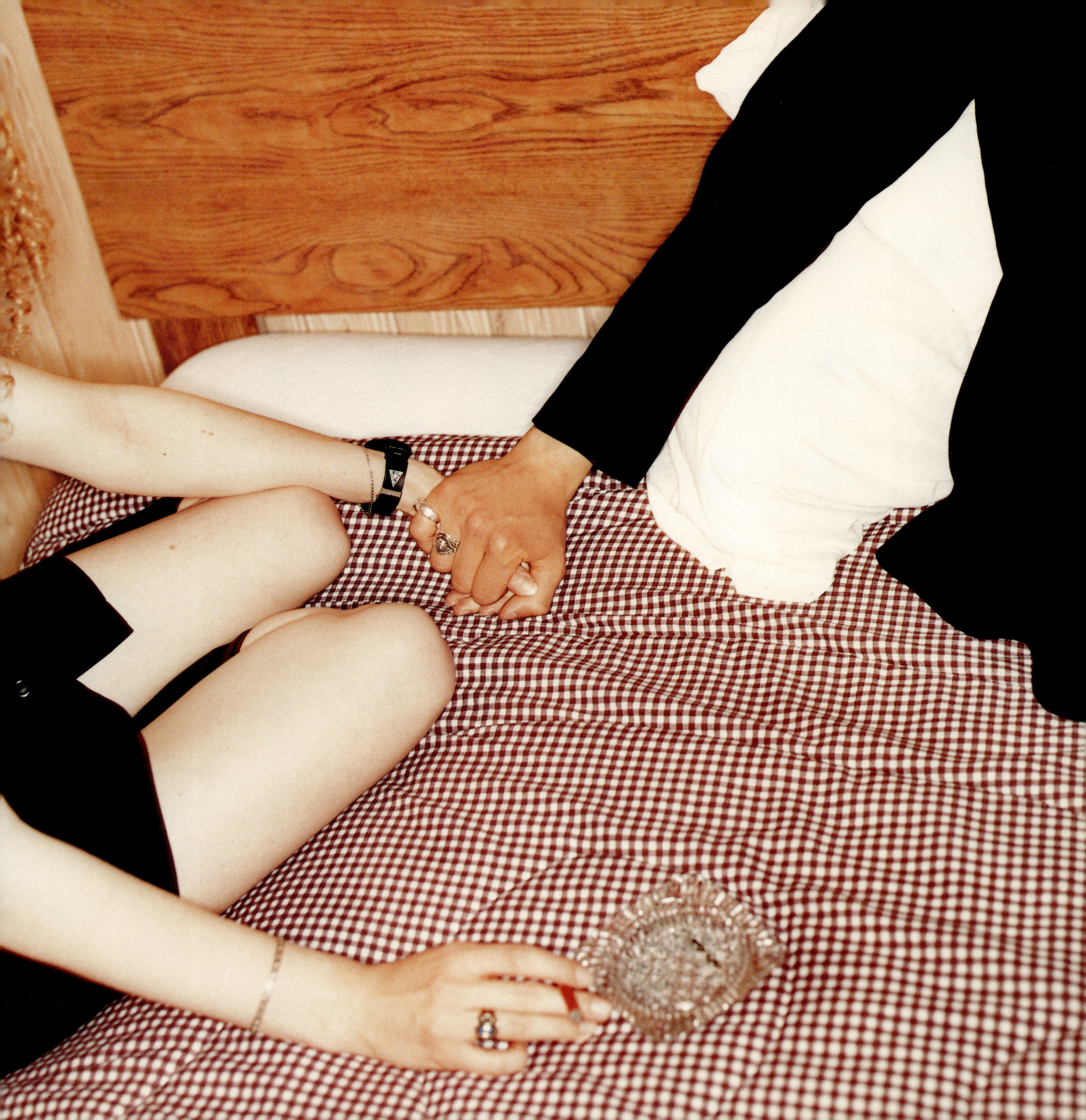

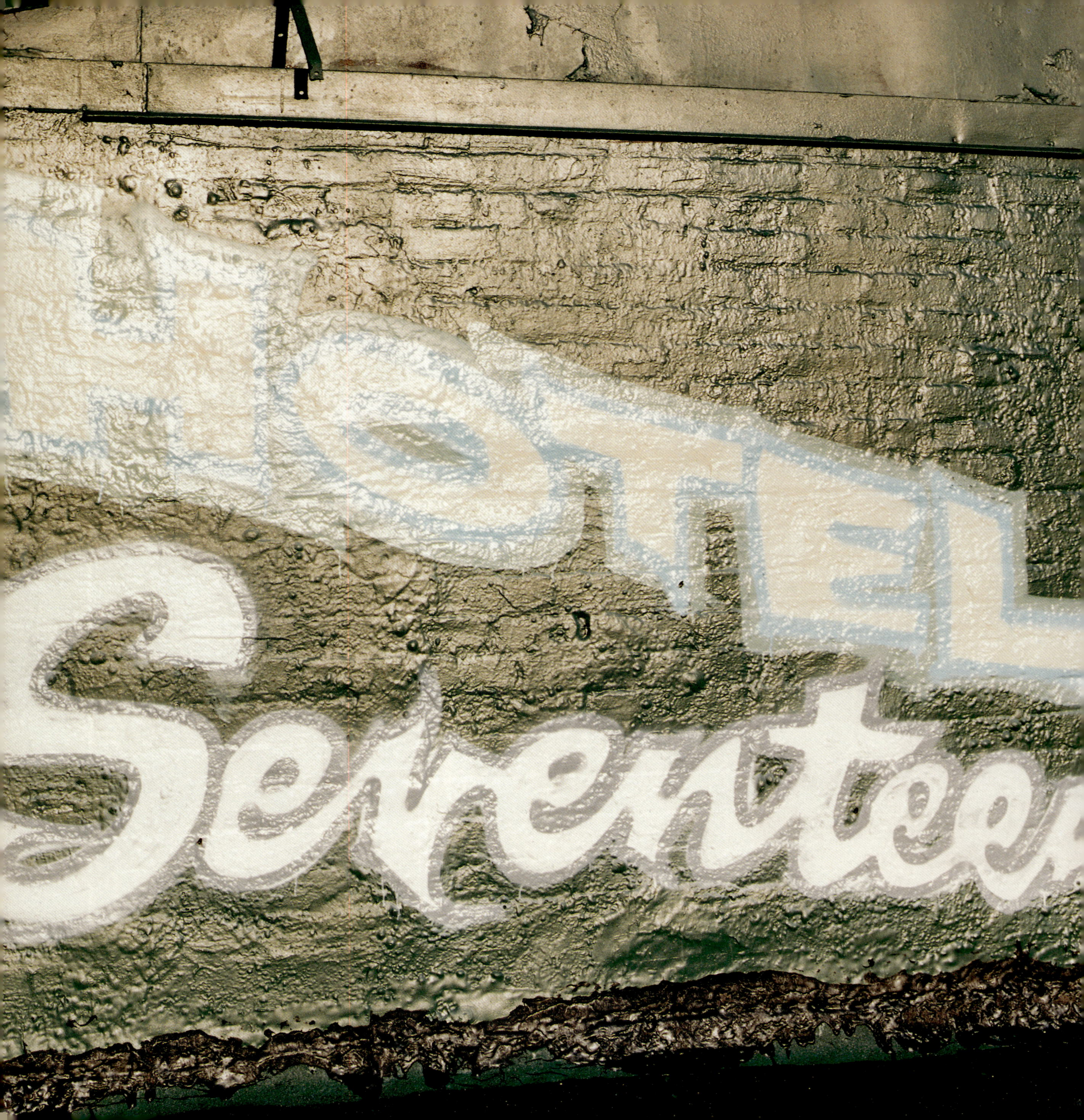
OTEL
Seventee

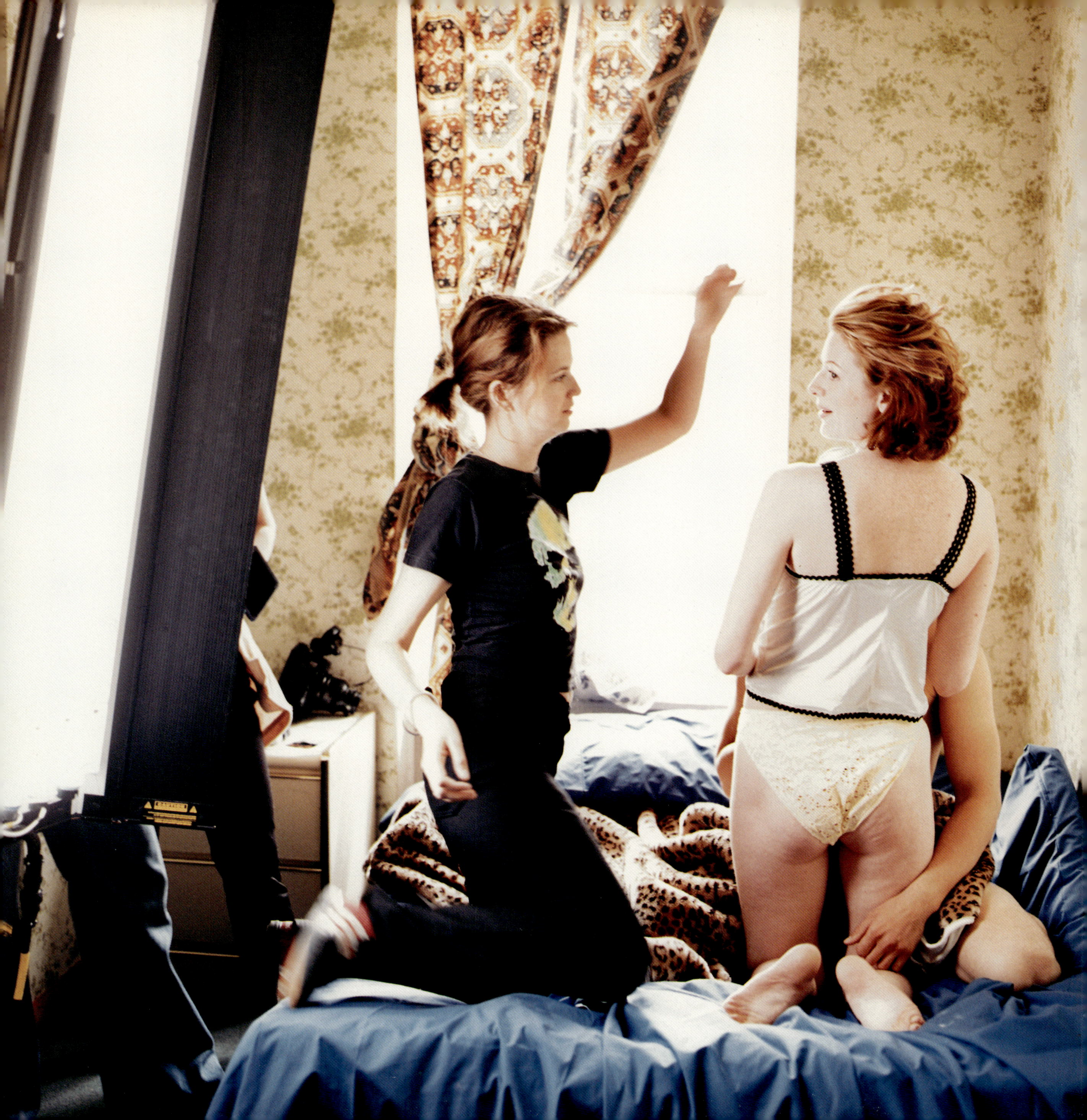

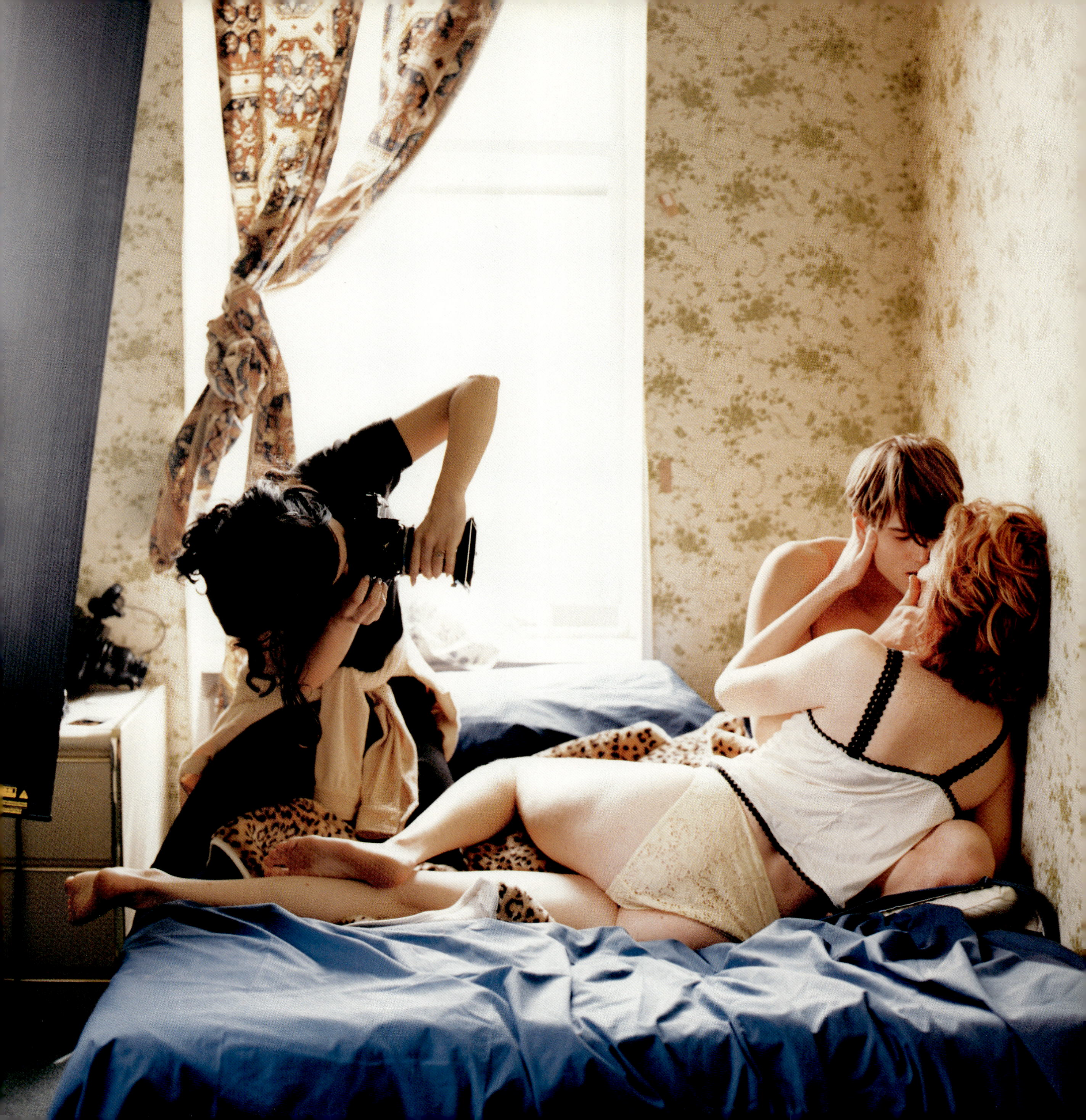

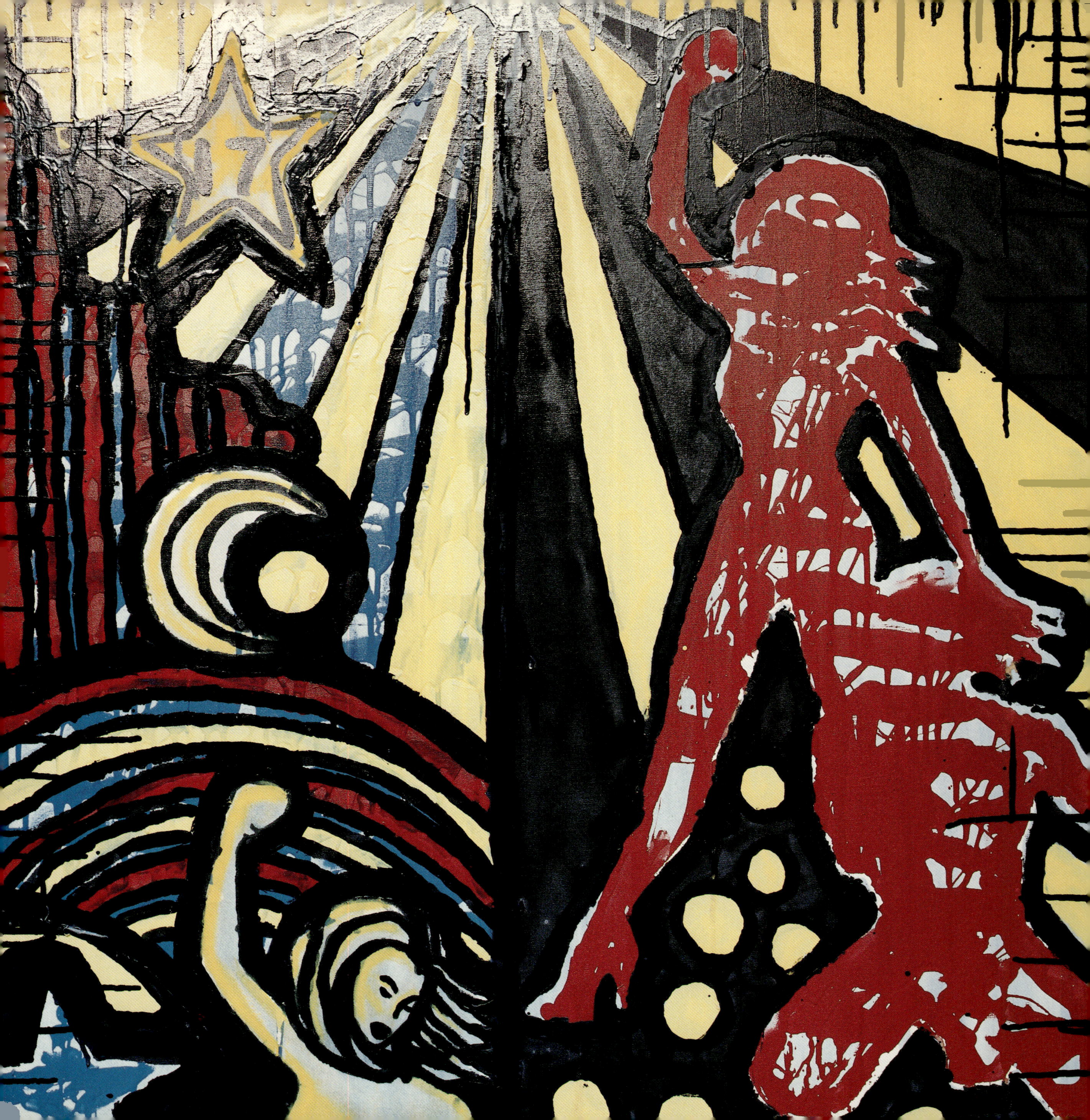

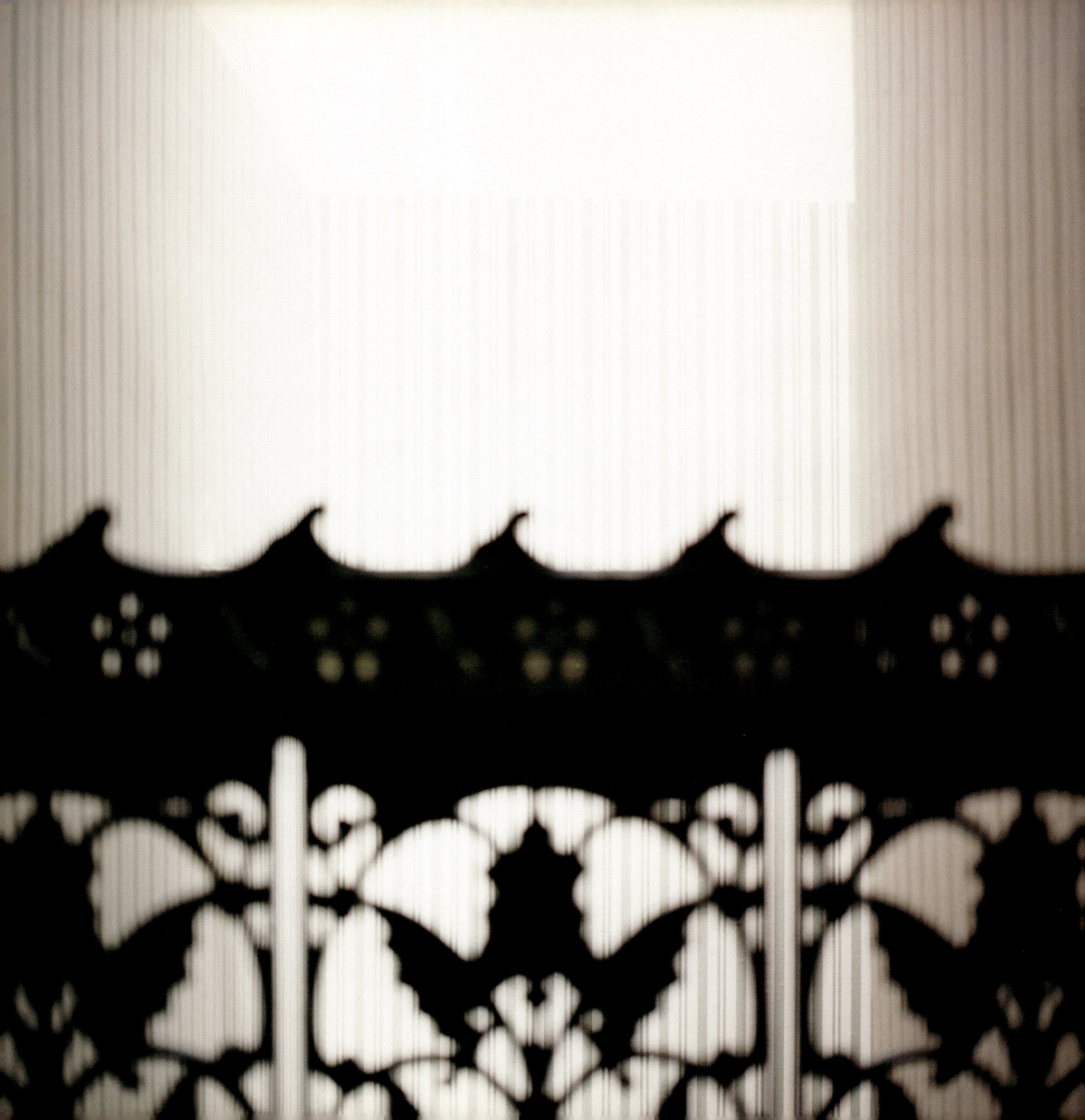

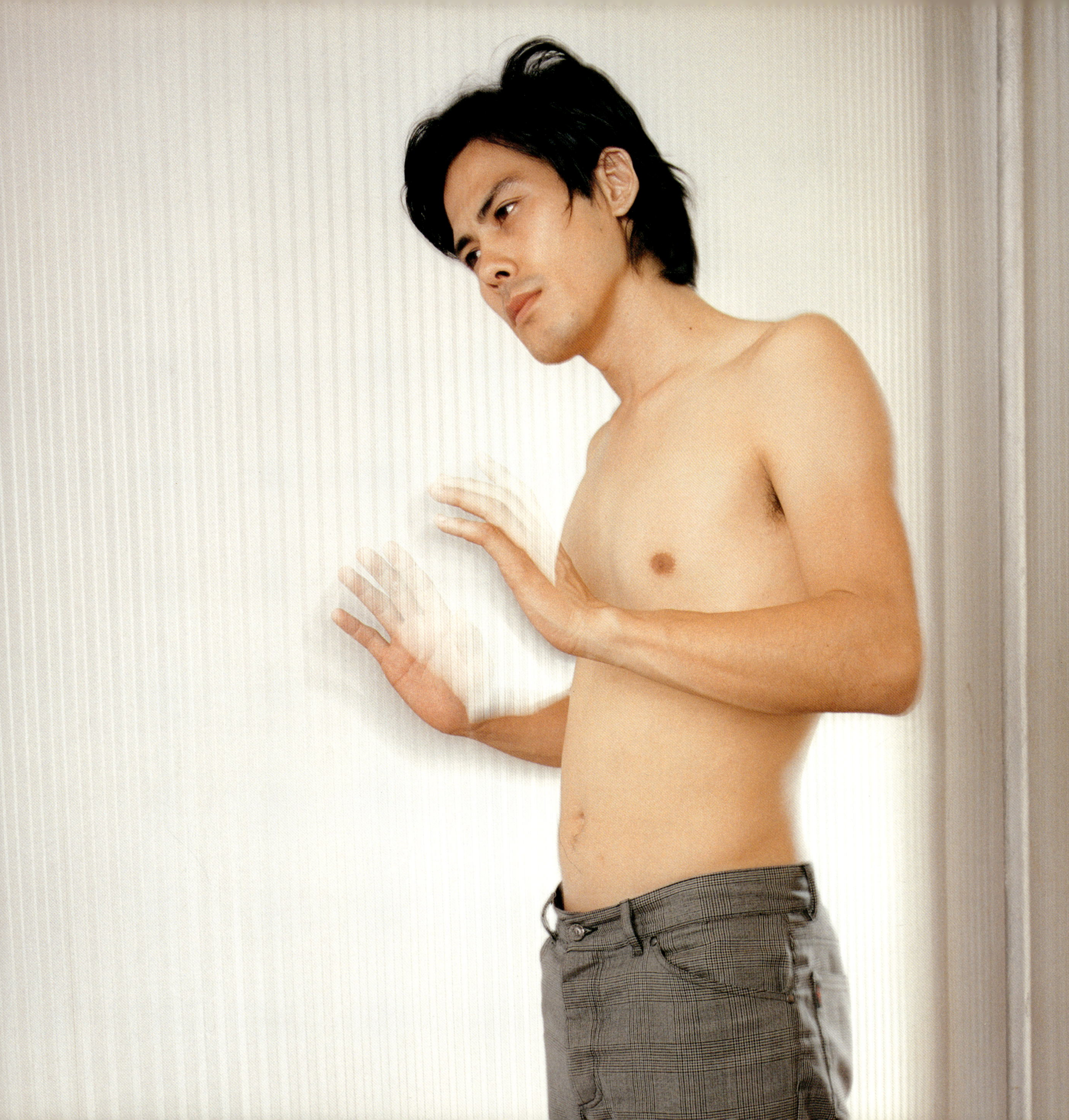

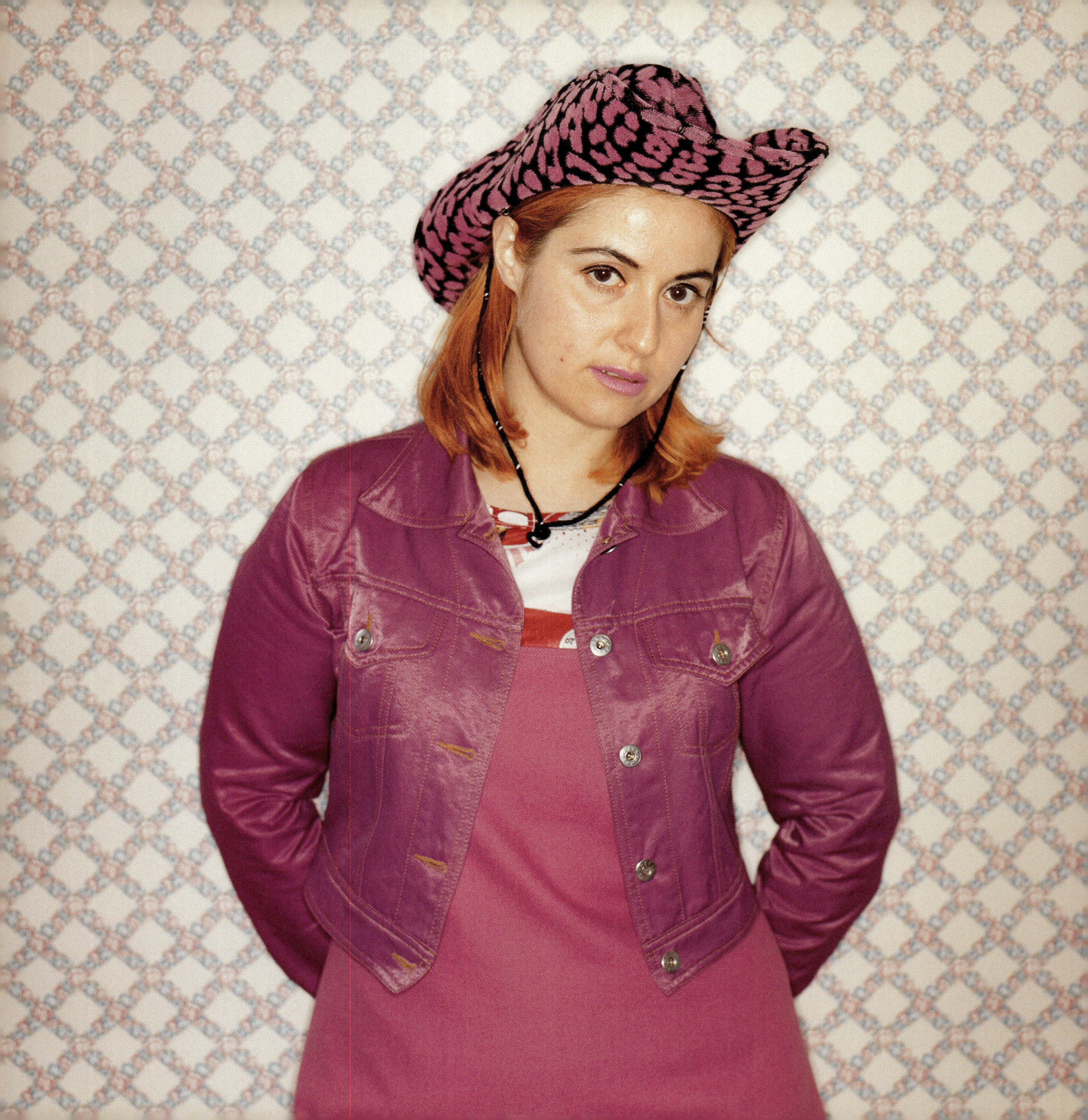

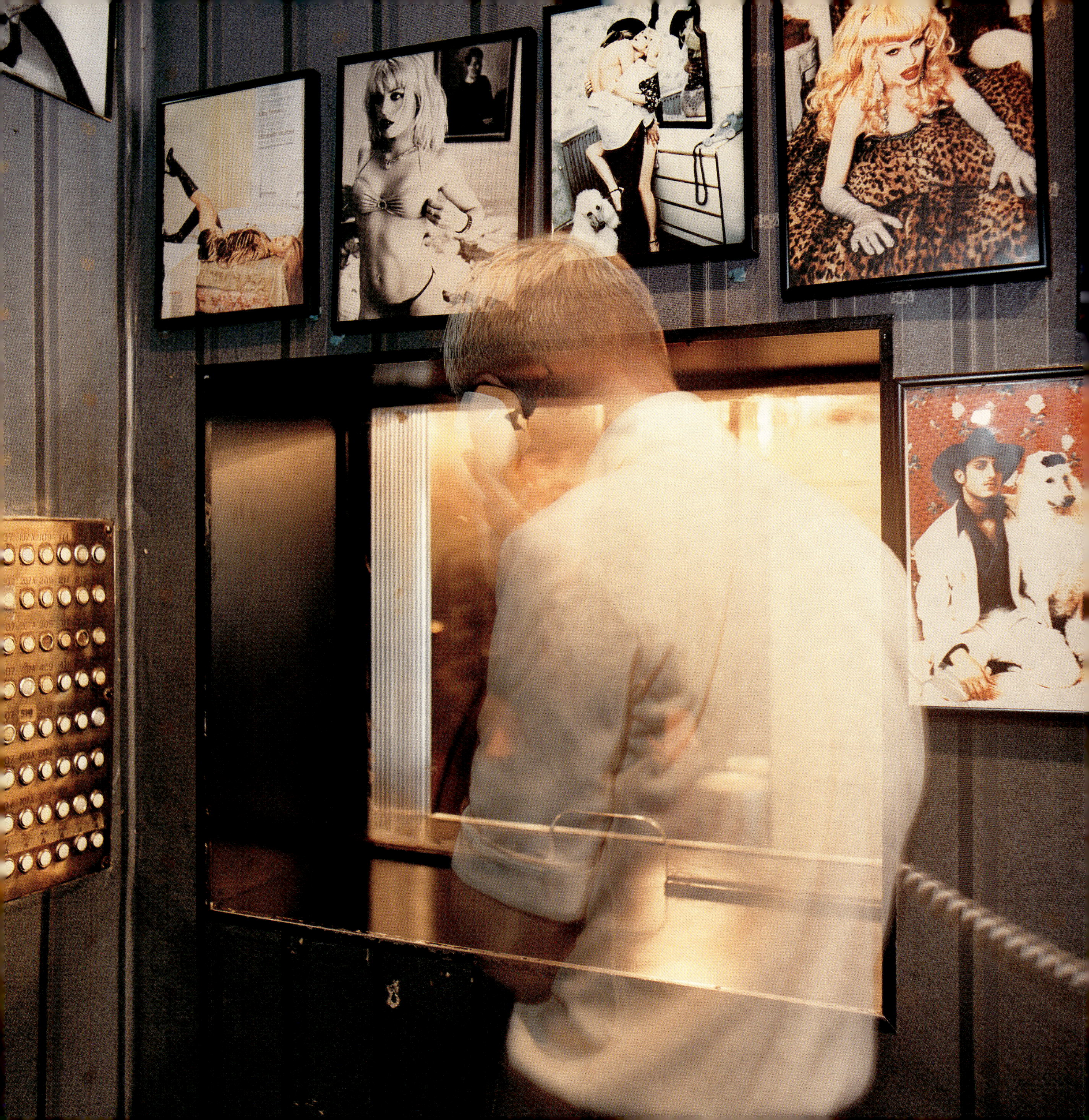

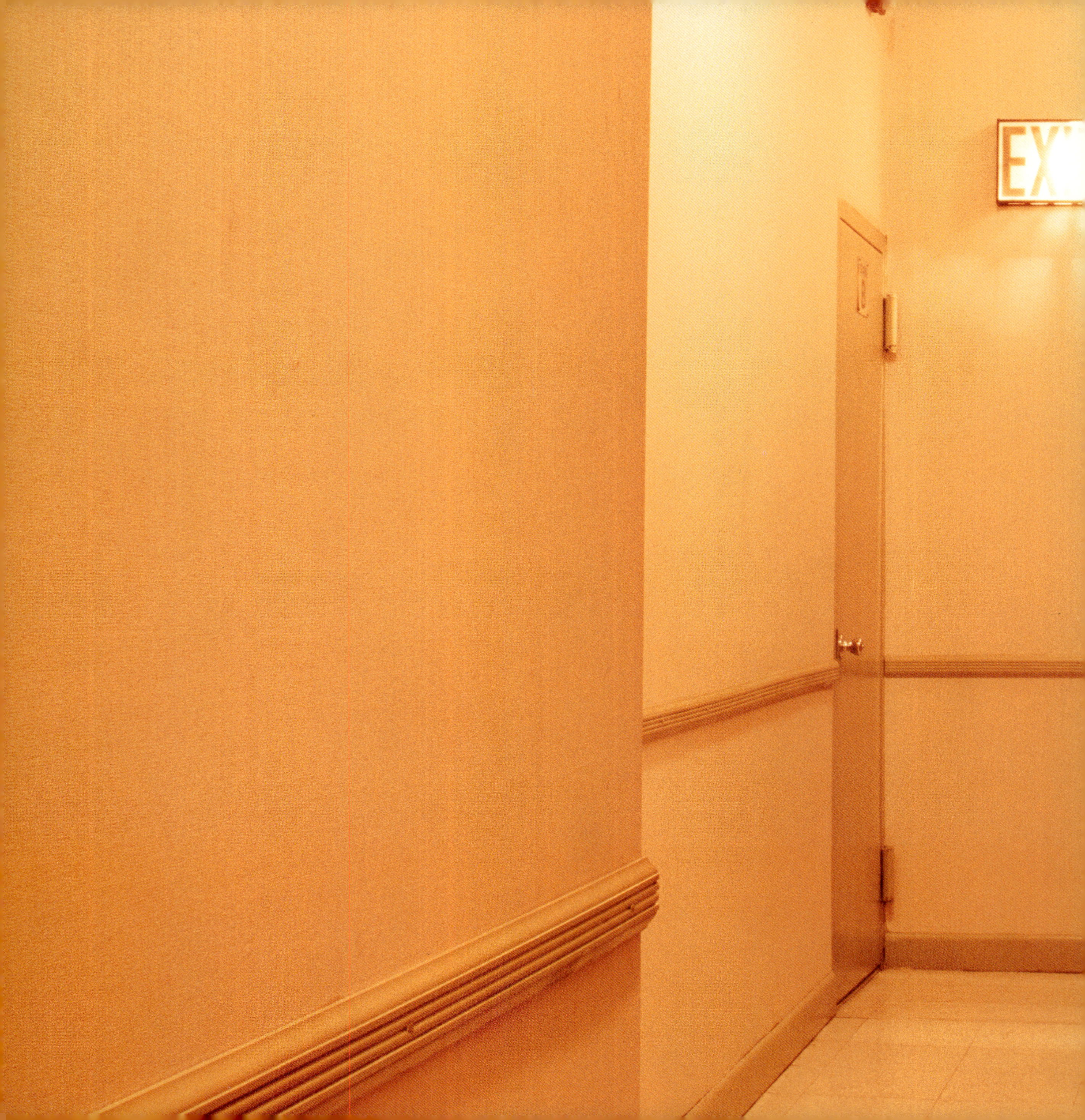

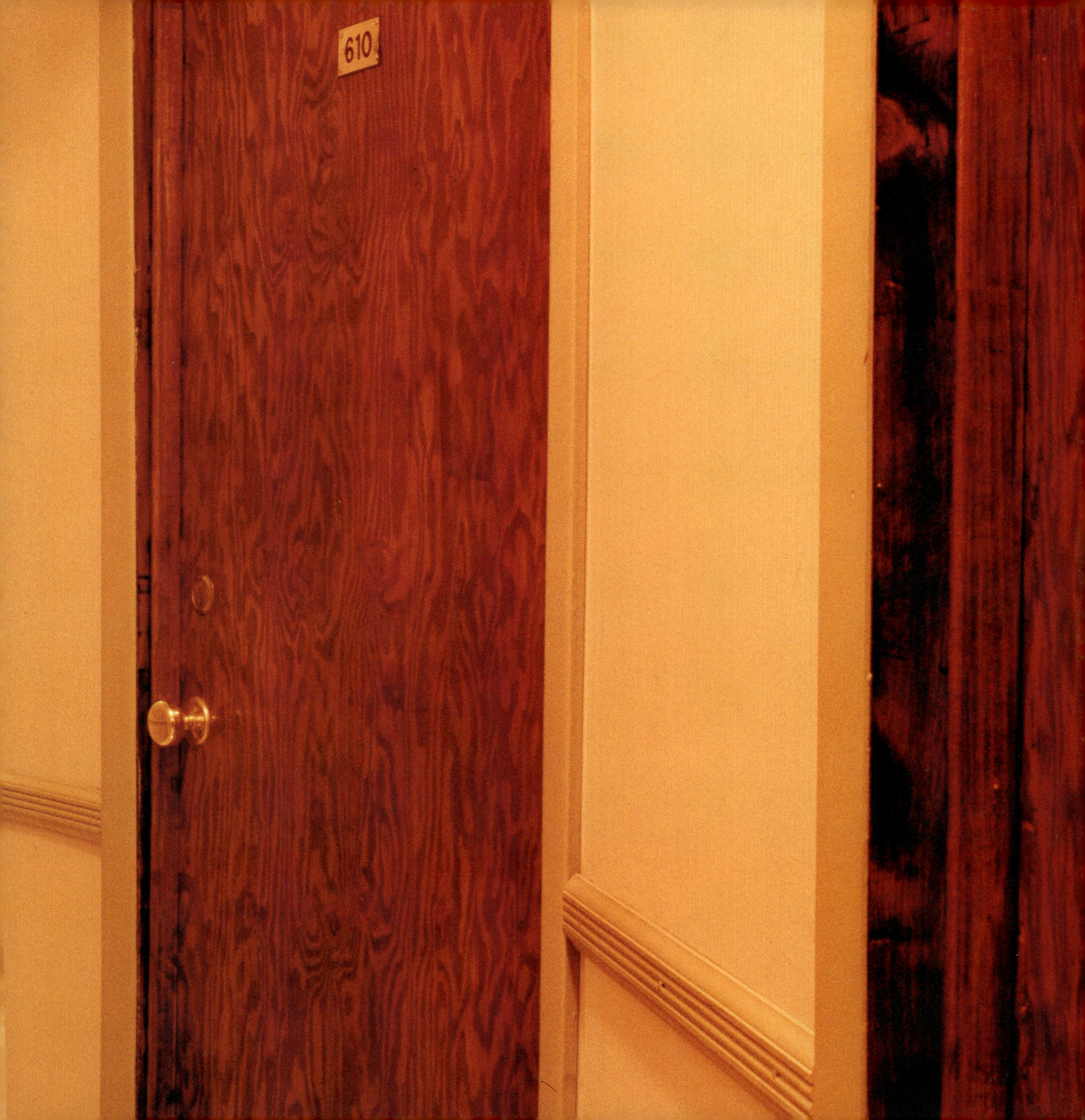
610

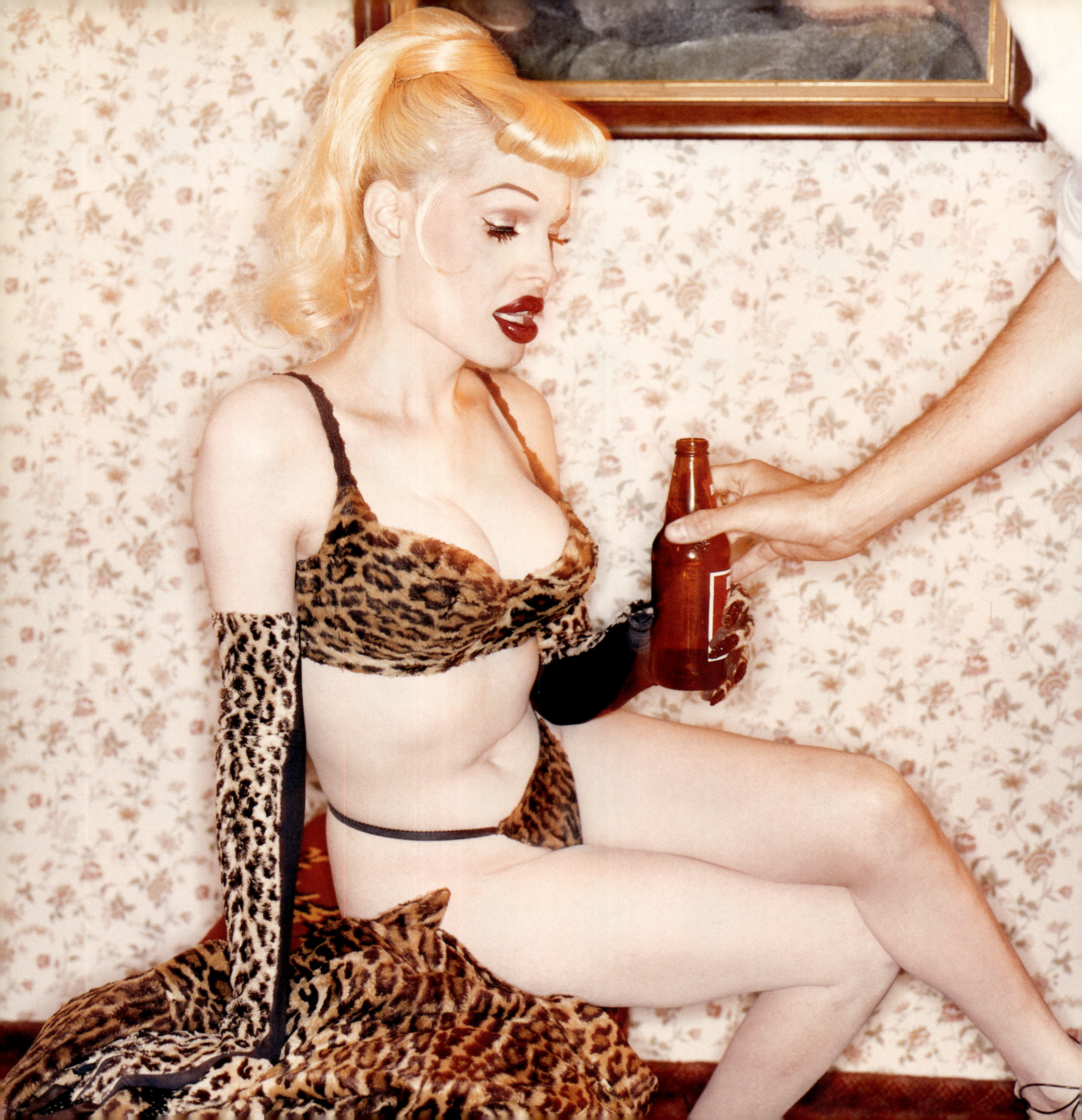

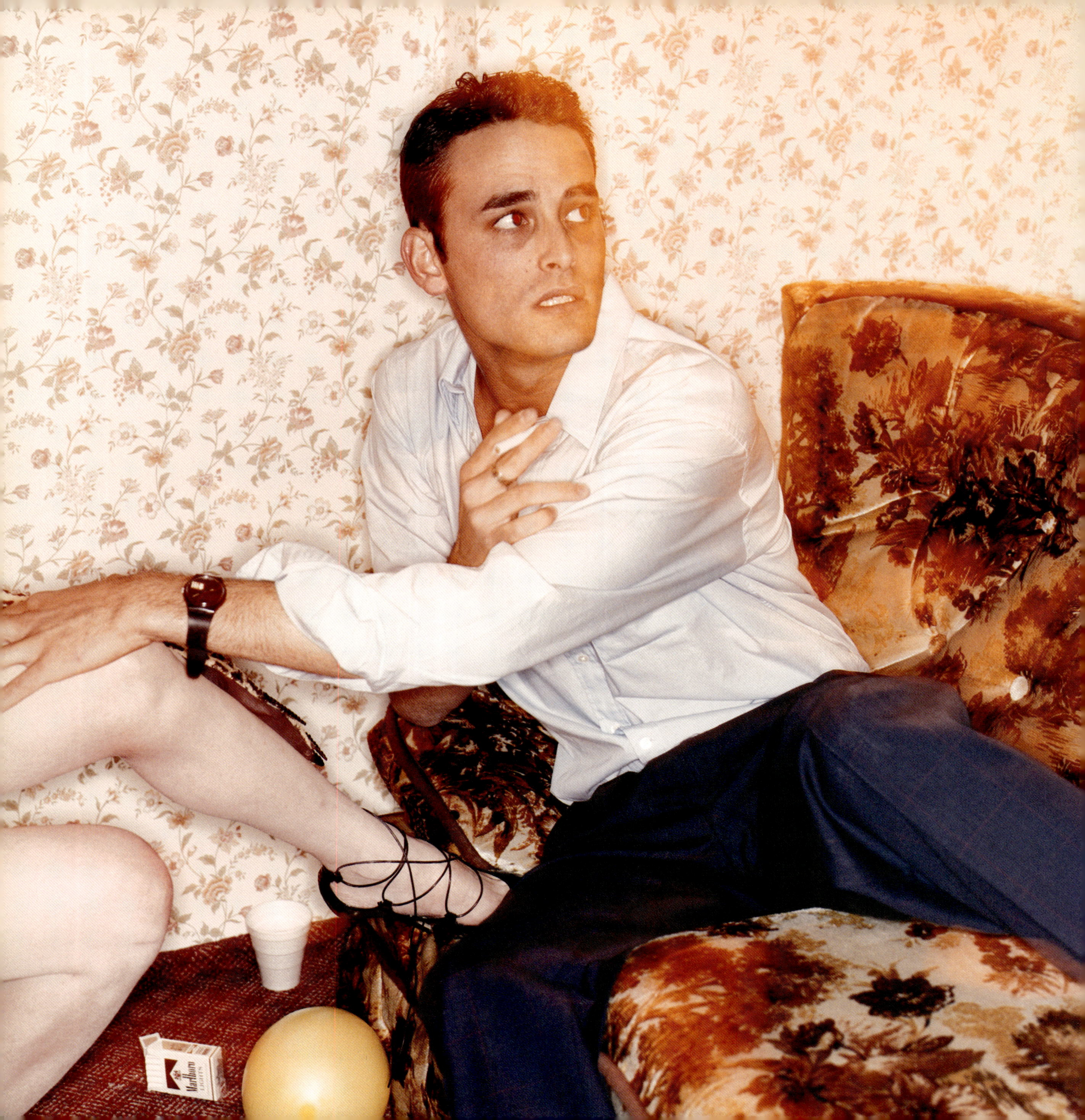
Marlboro

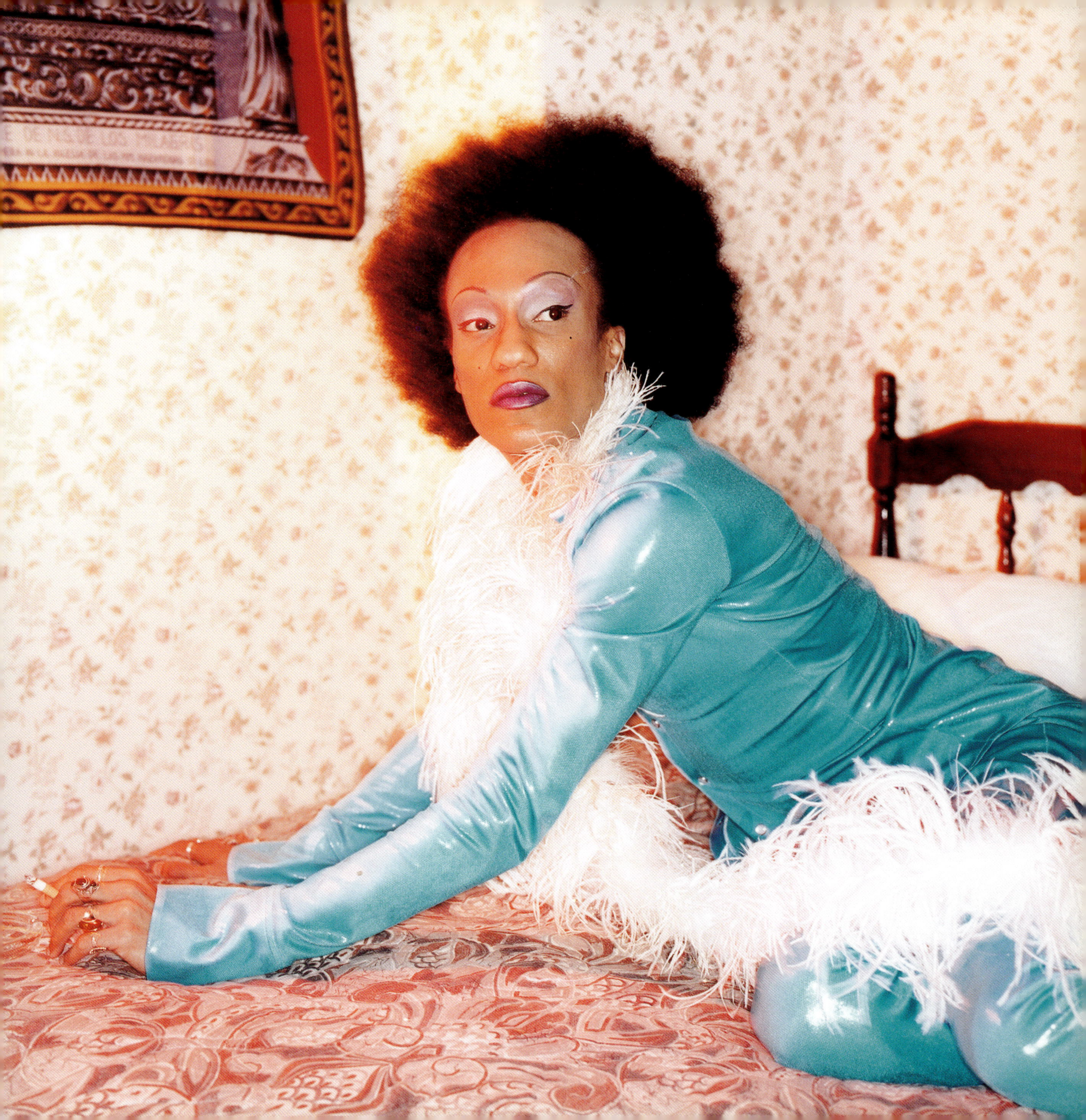

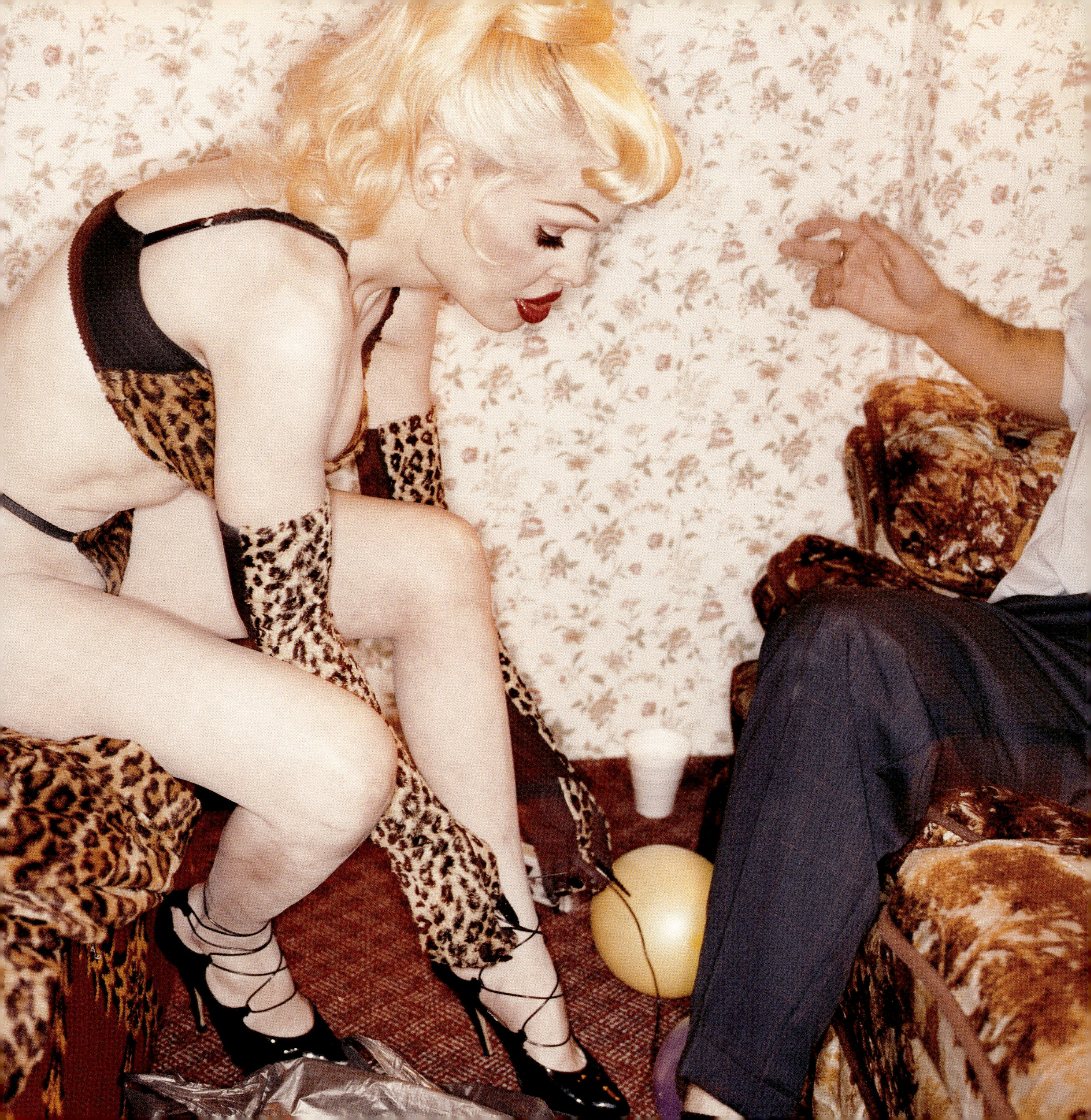

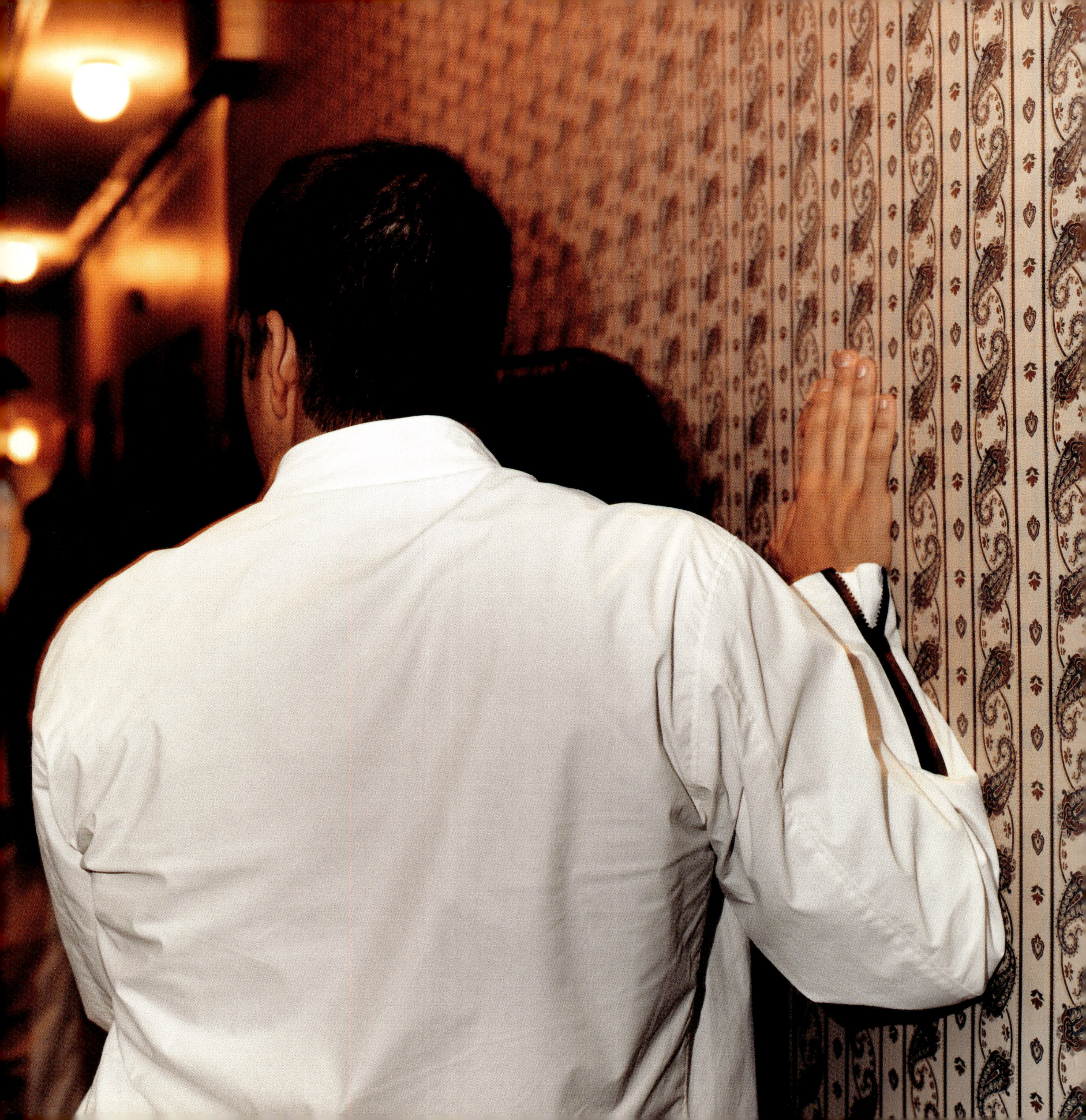

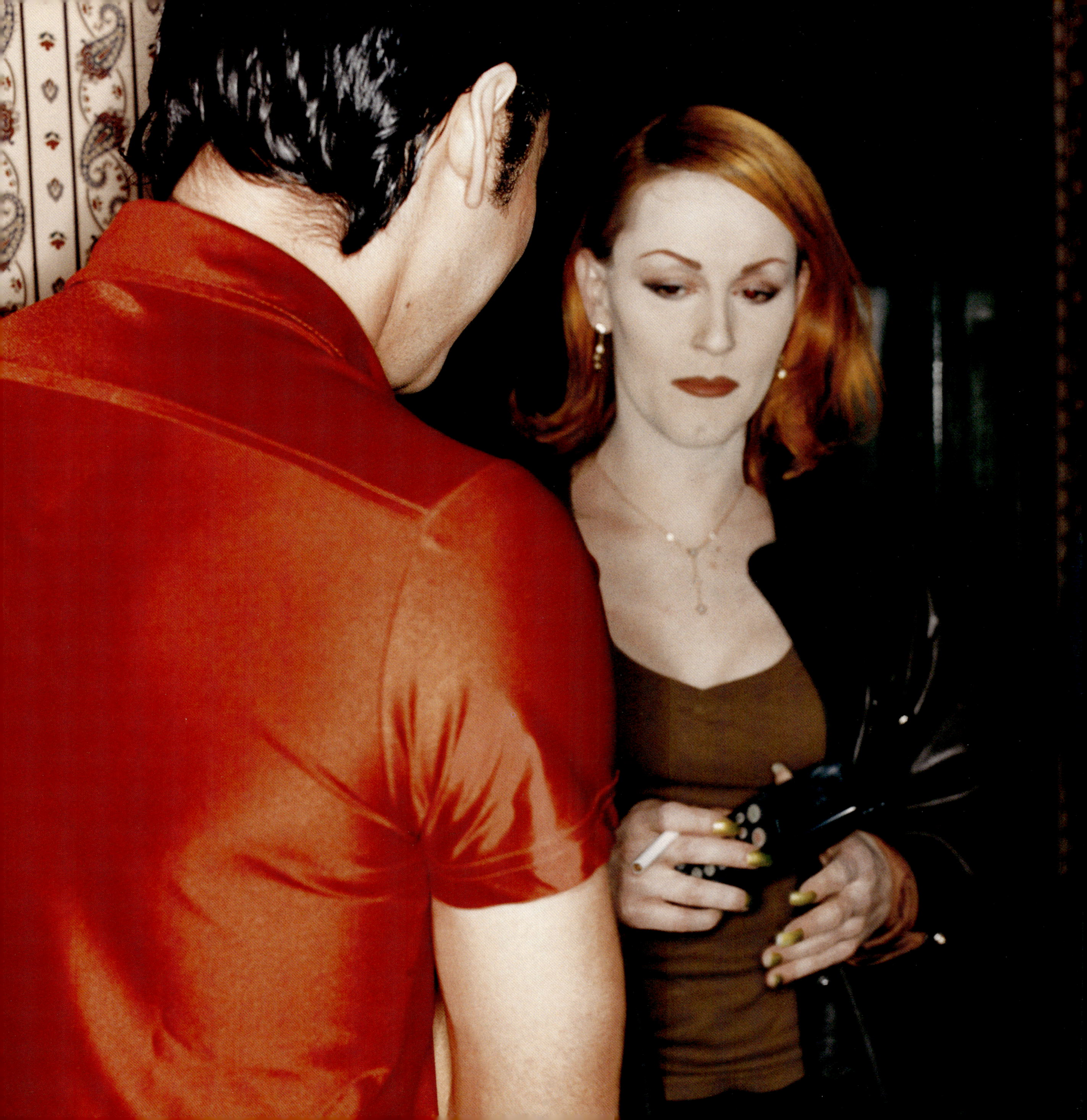

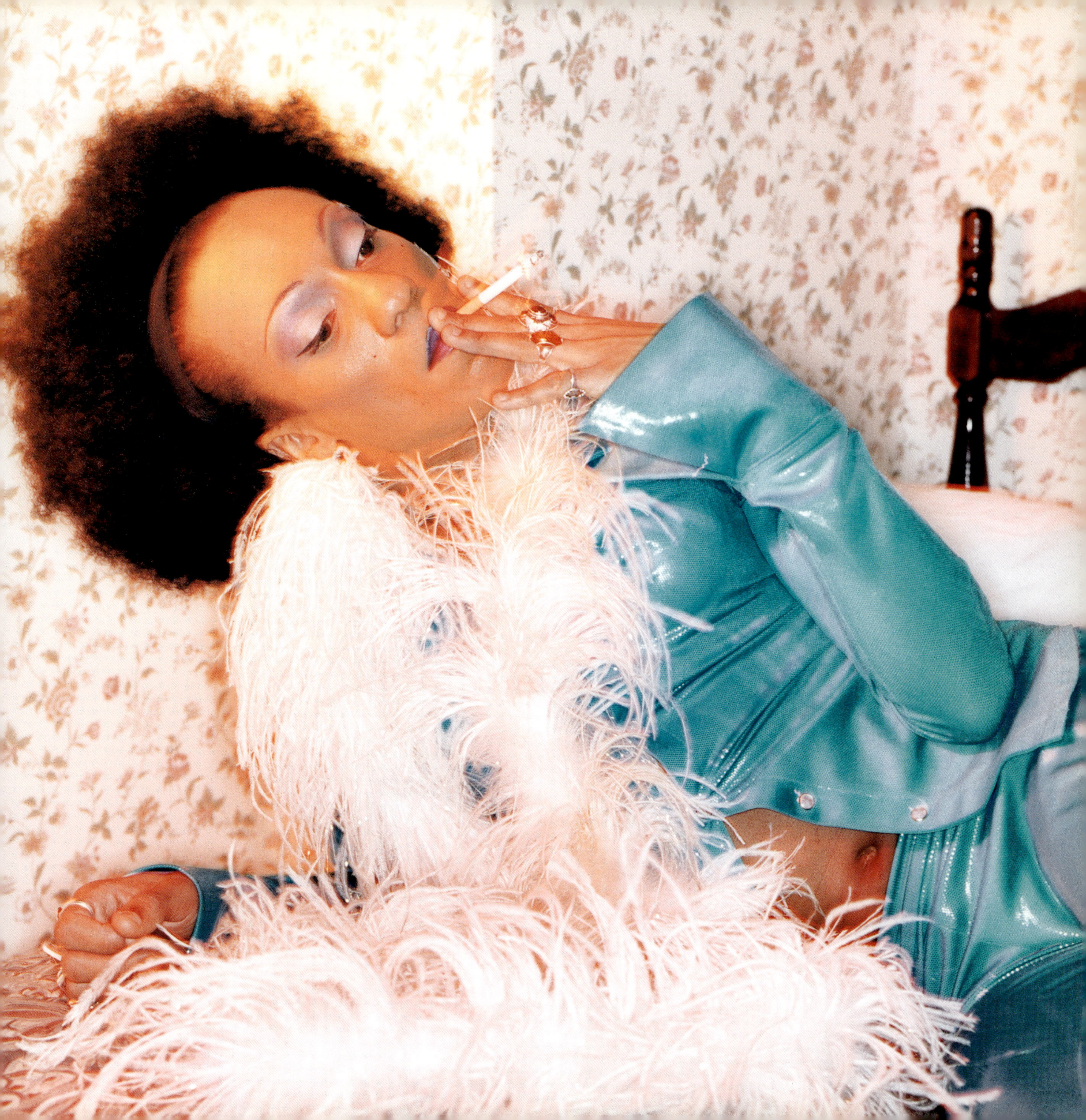

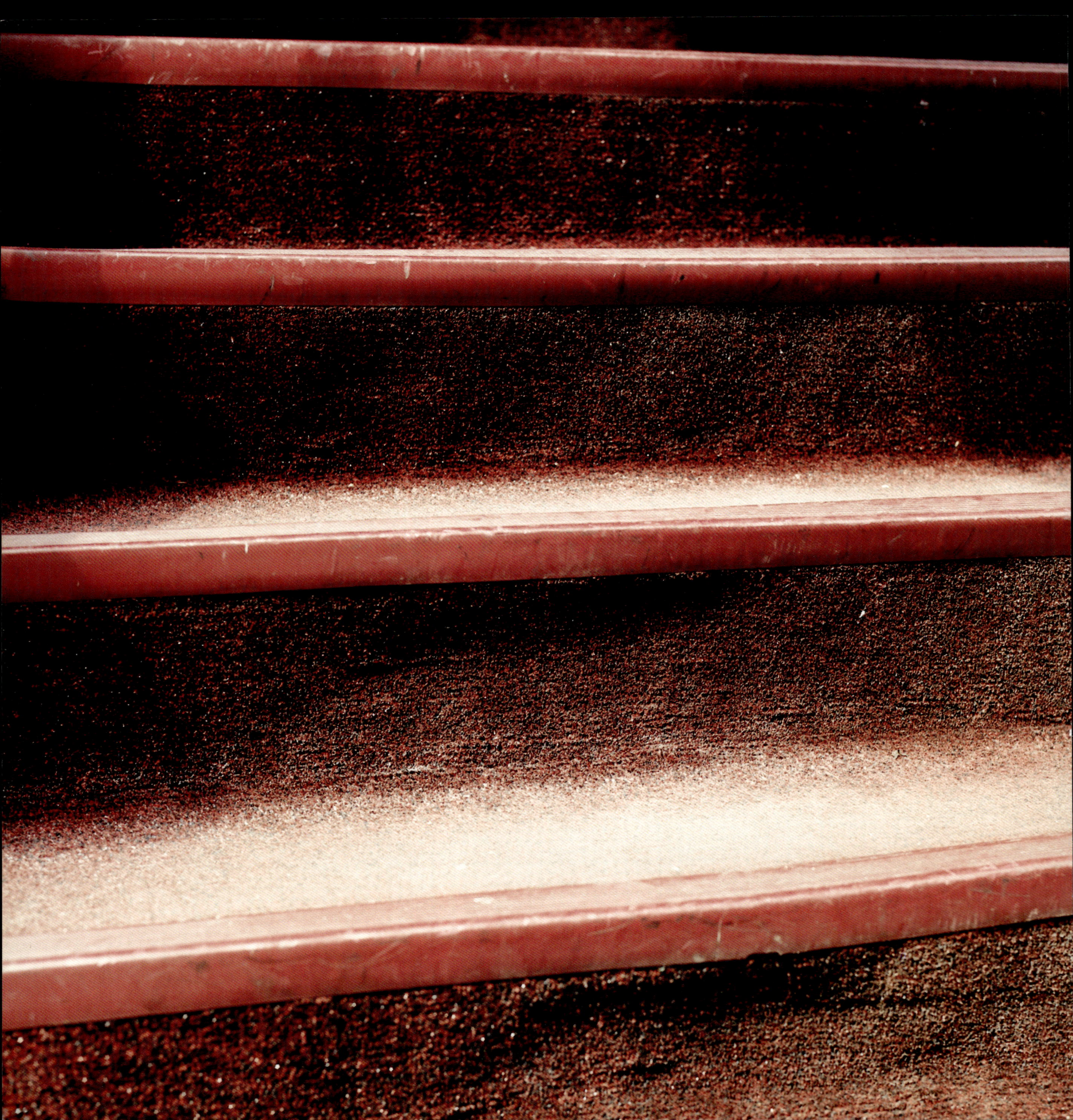

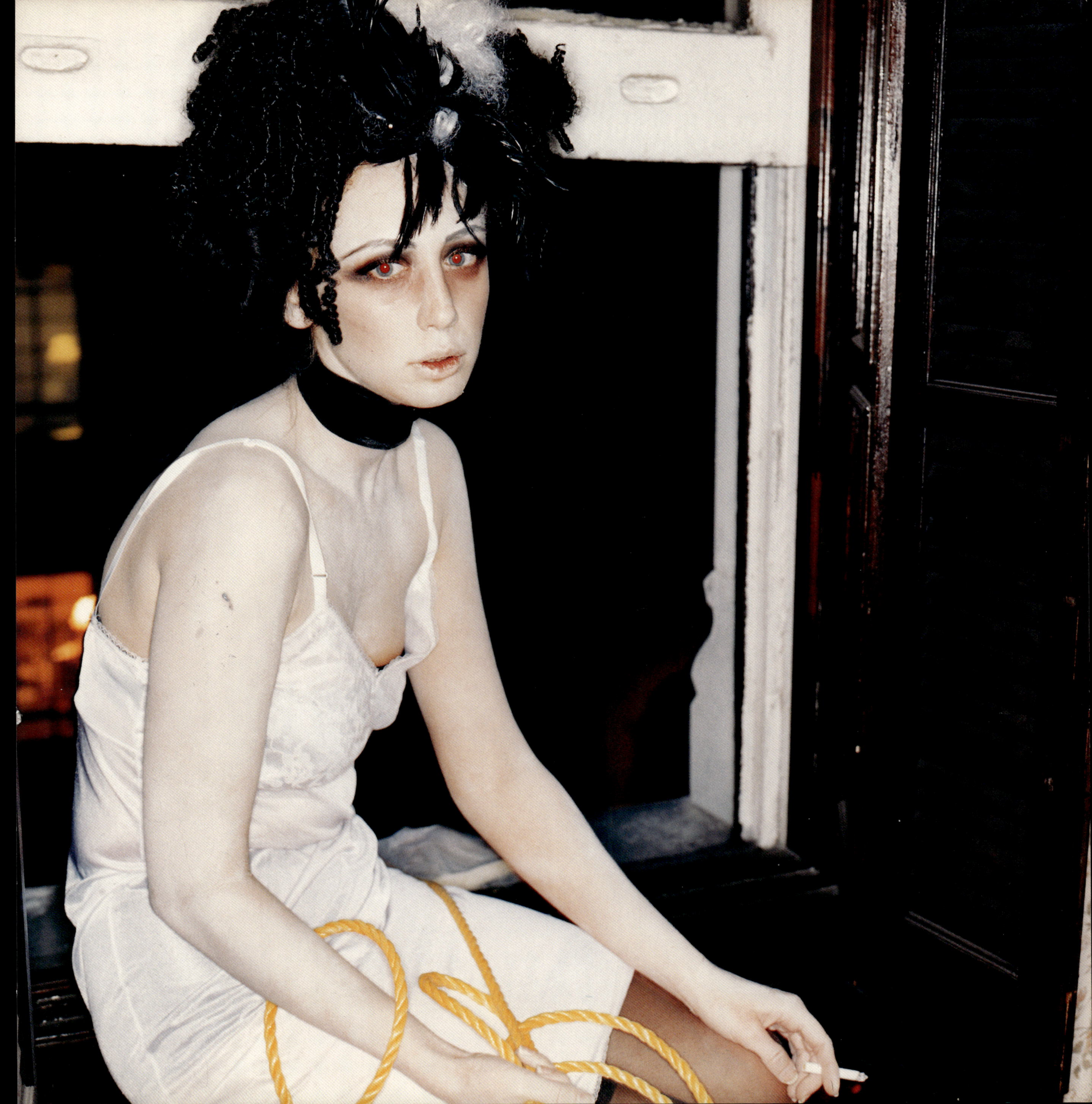

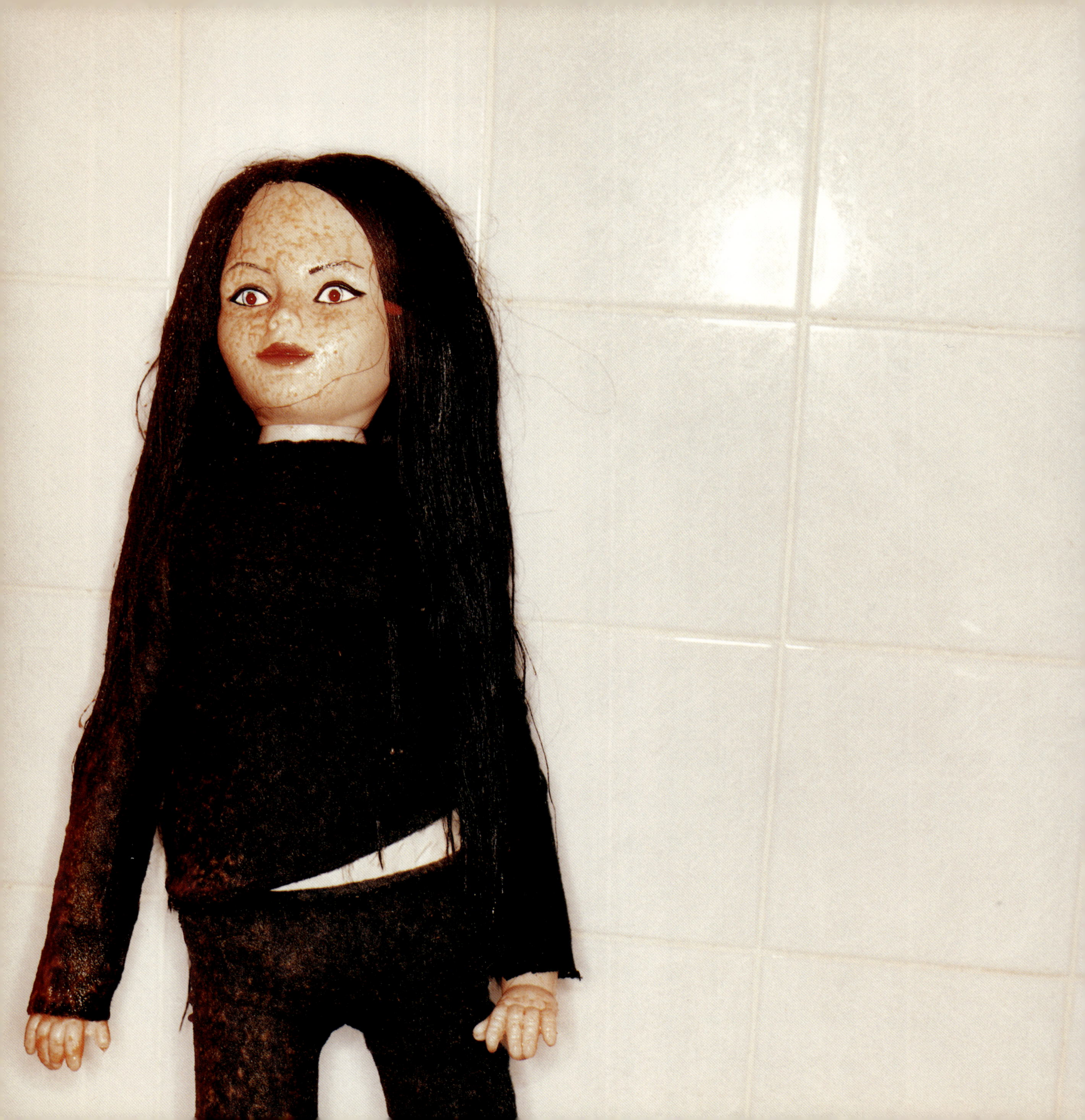

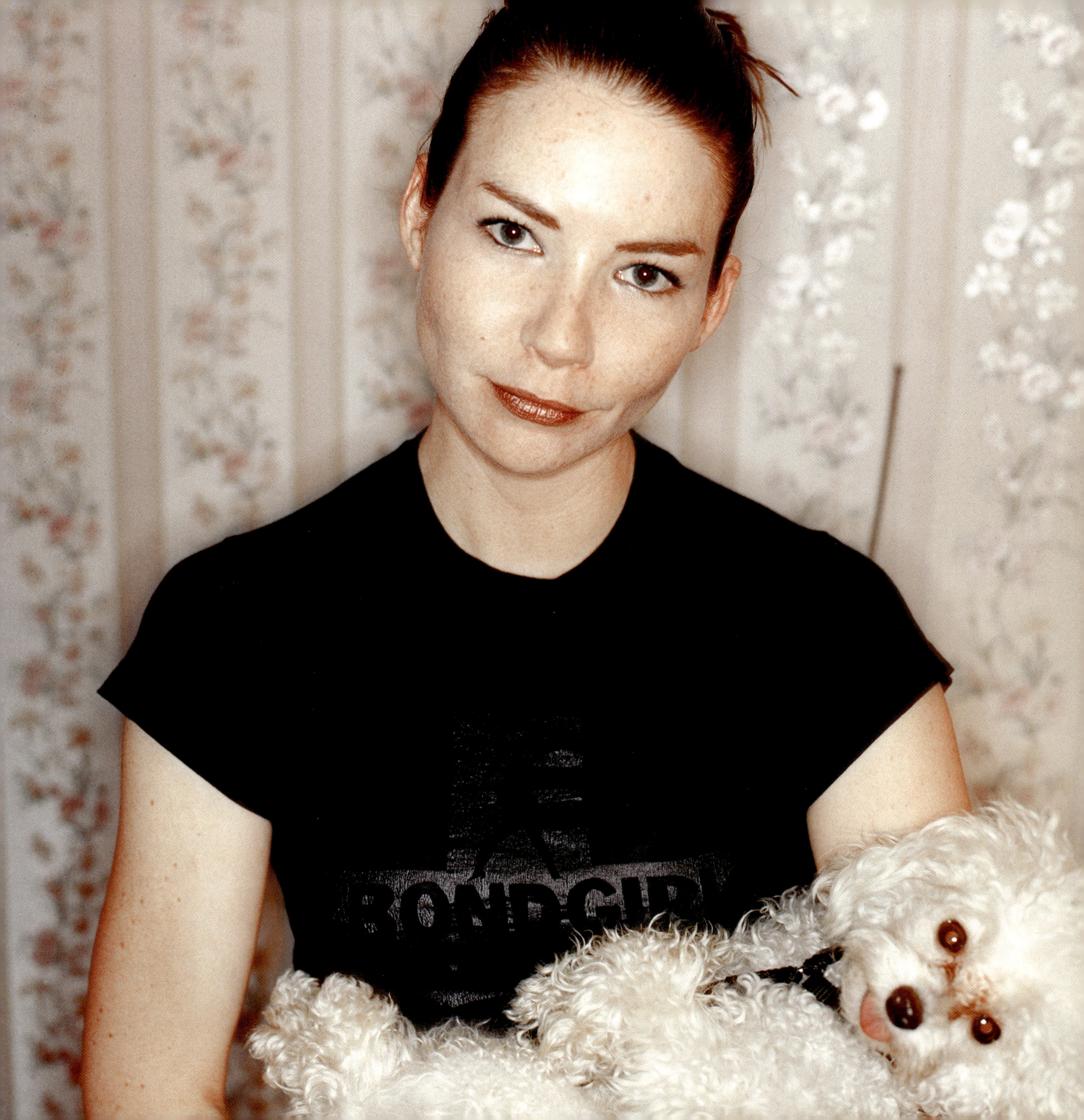

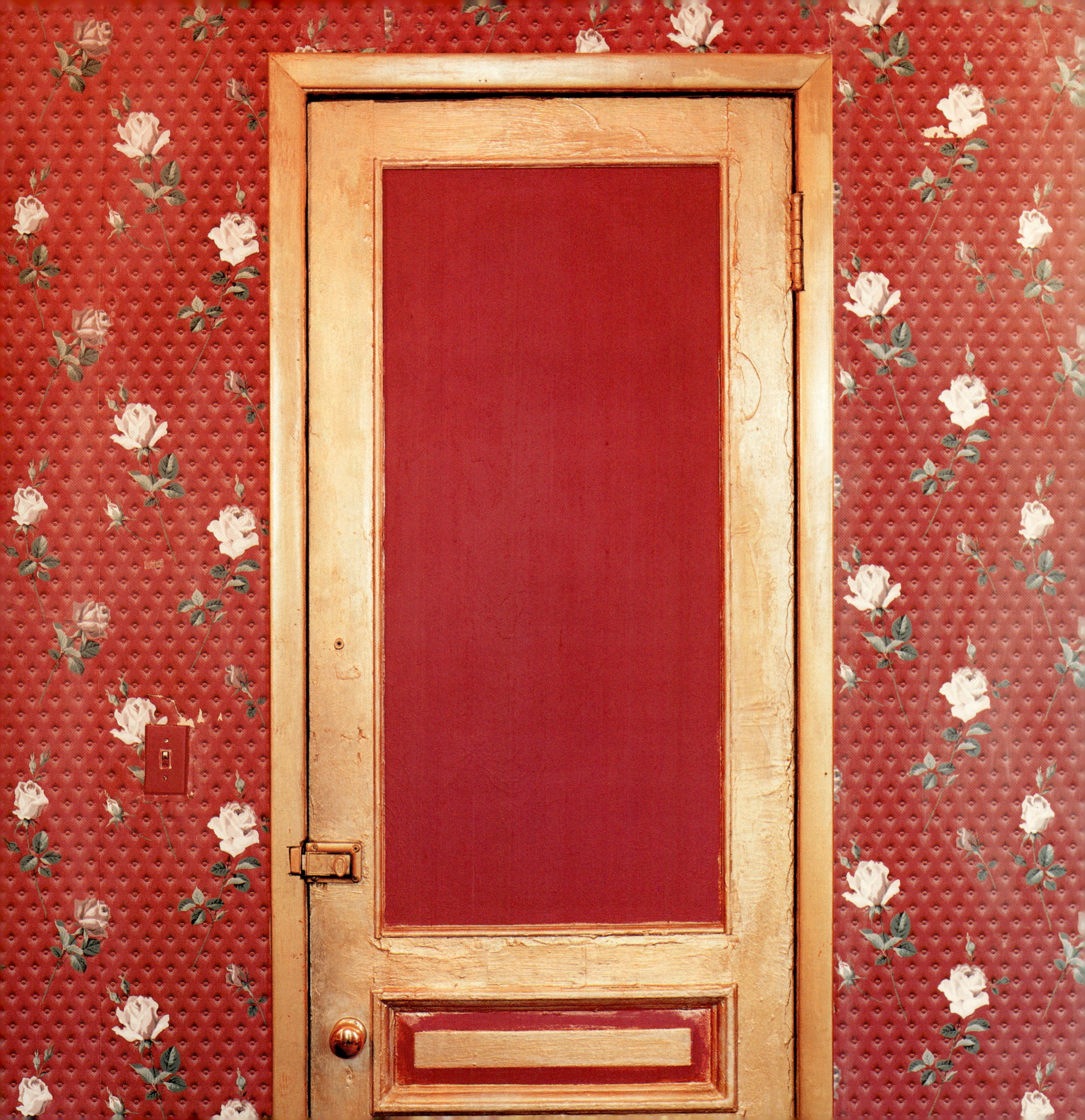

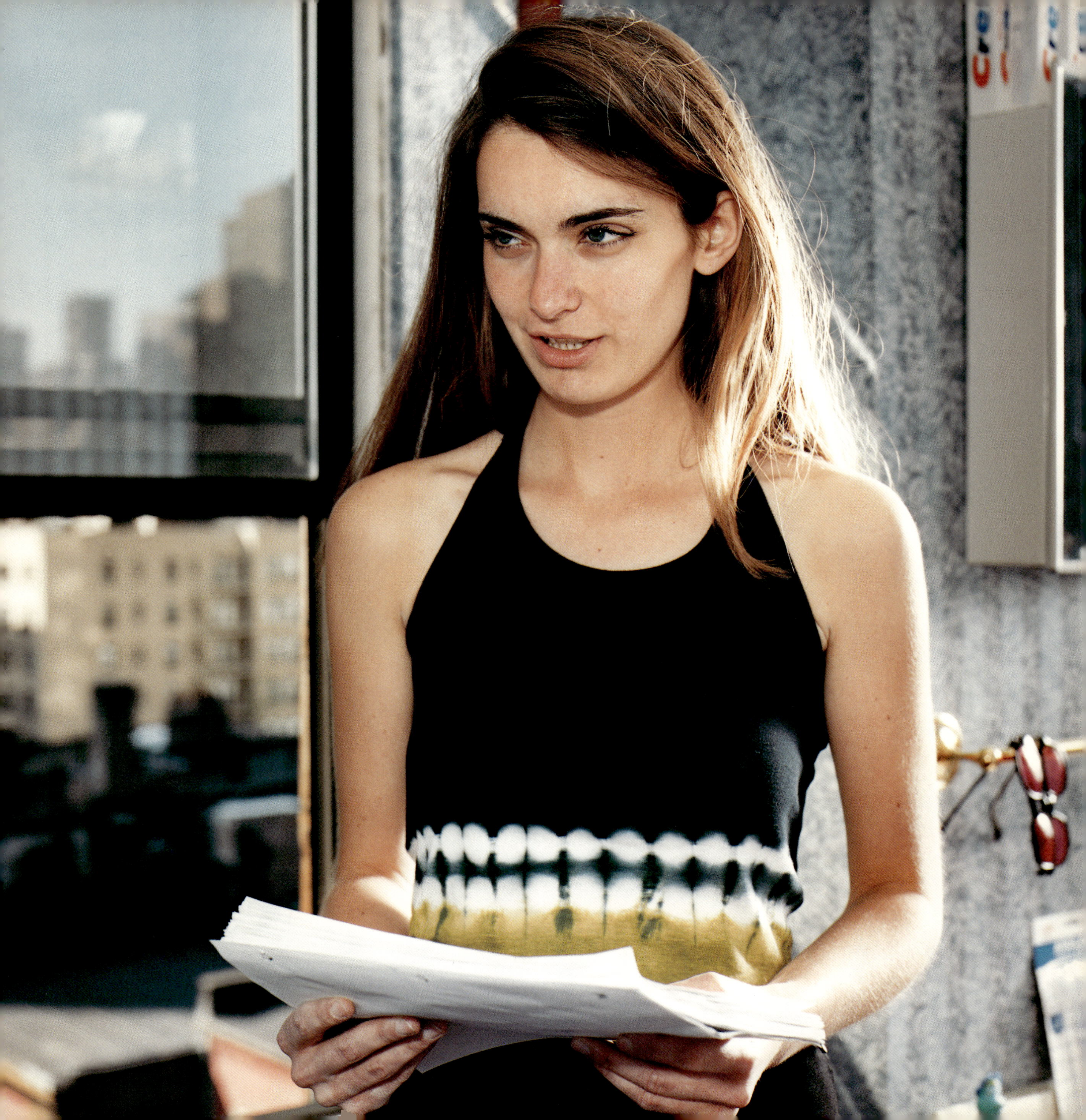

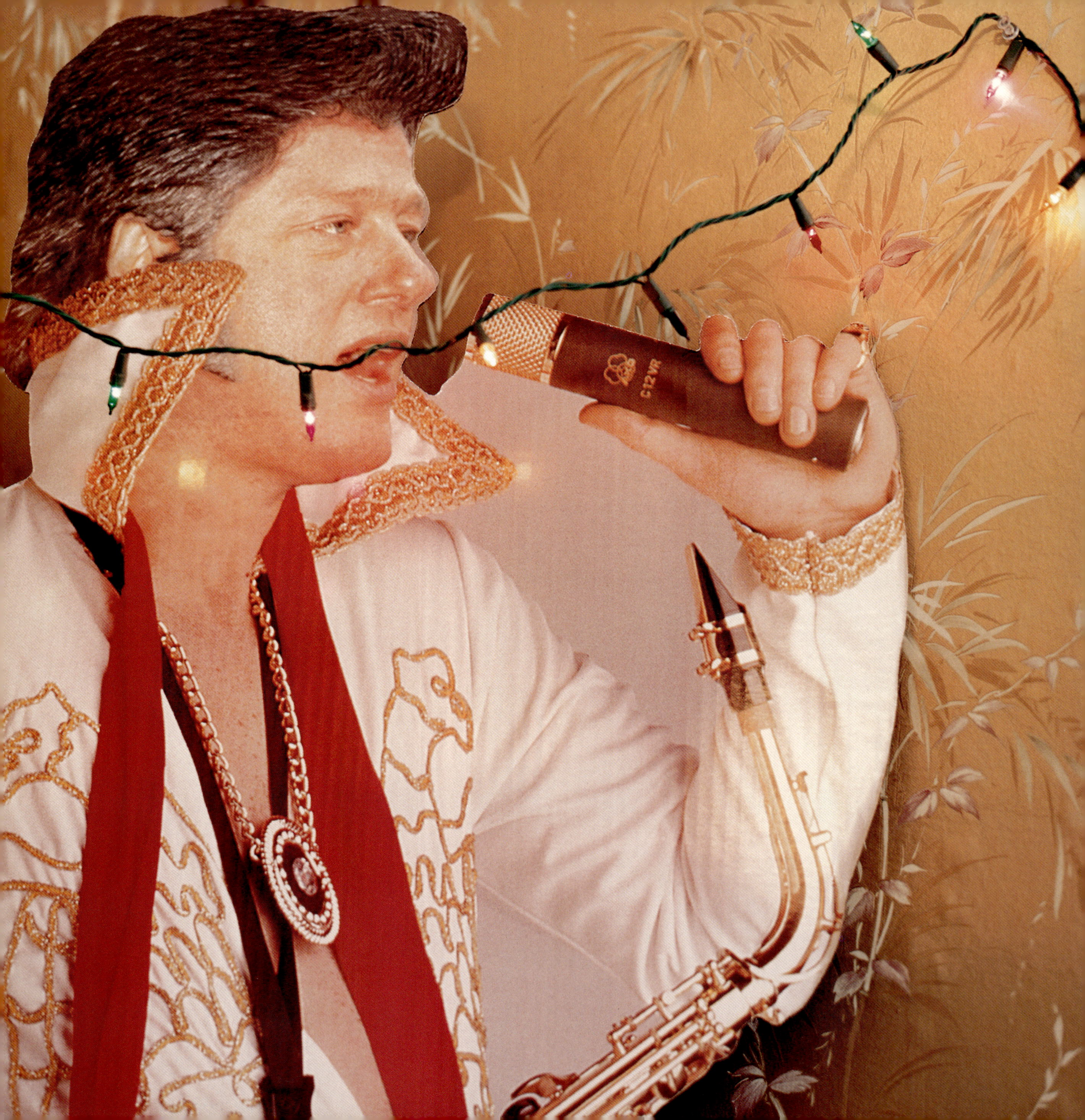
C12VR

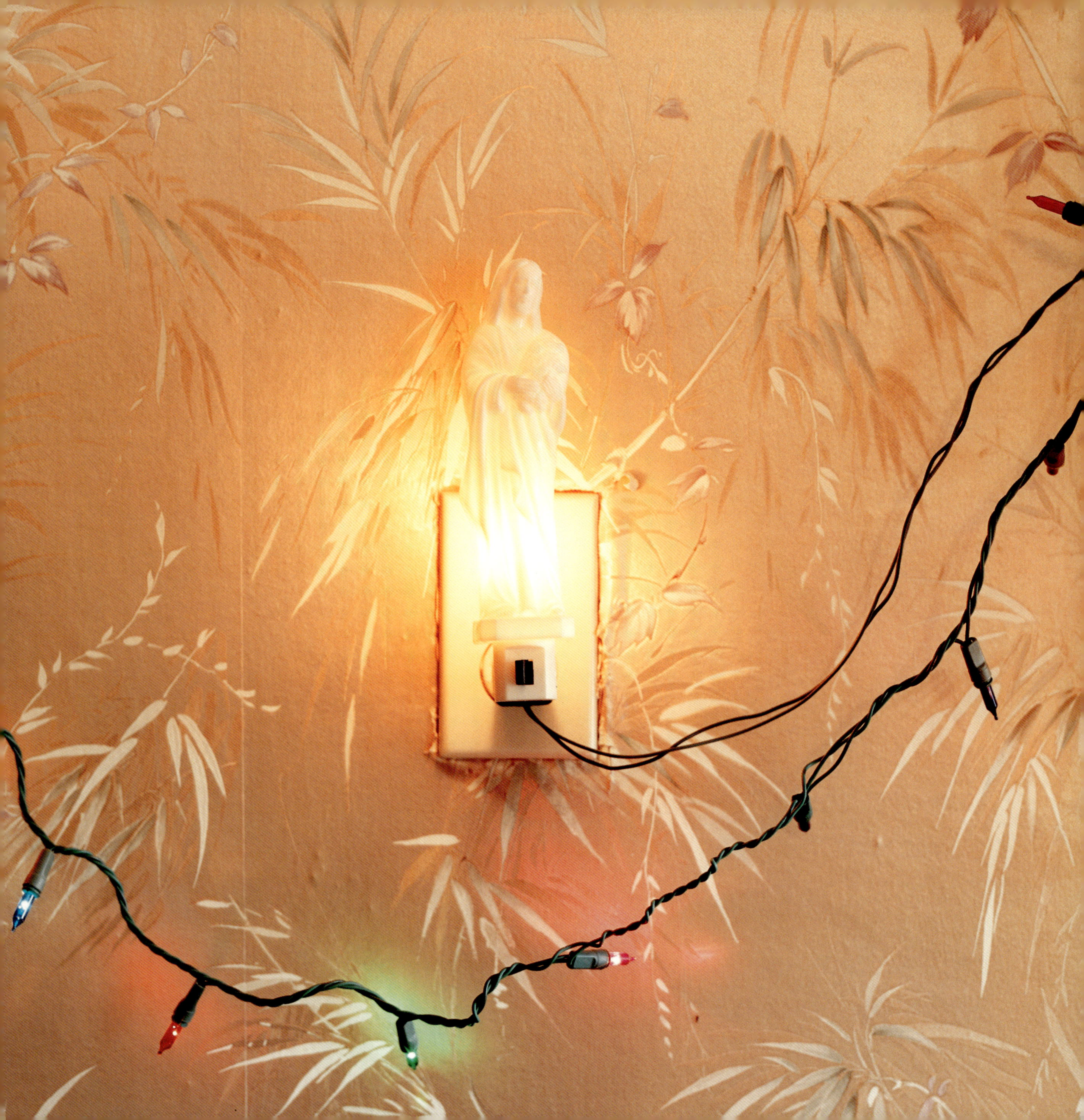

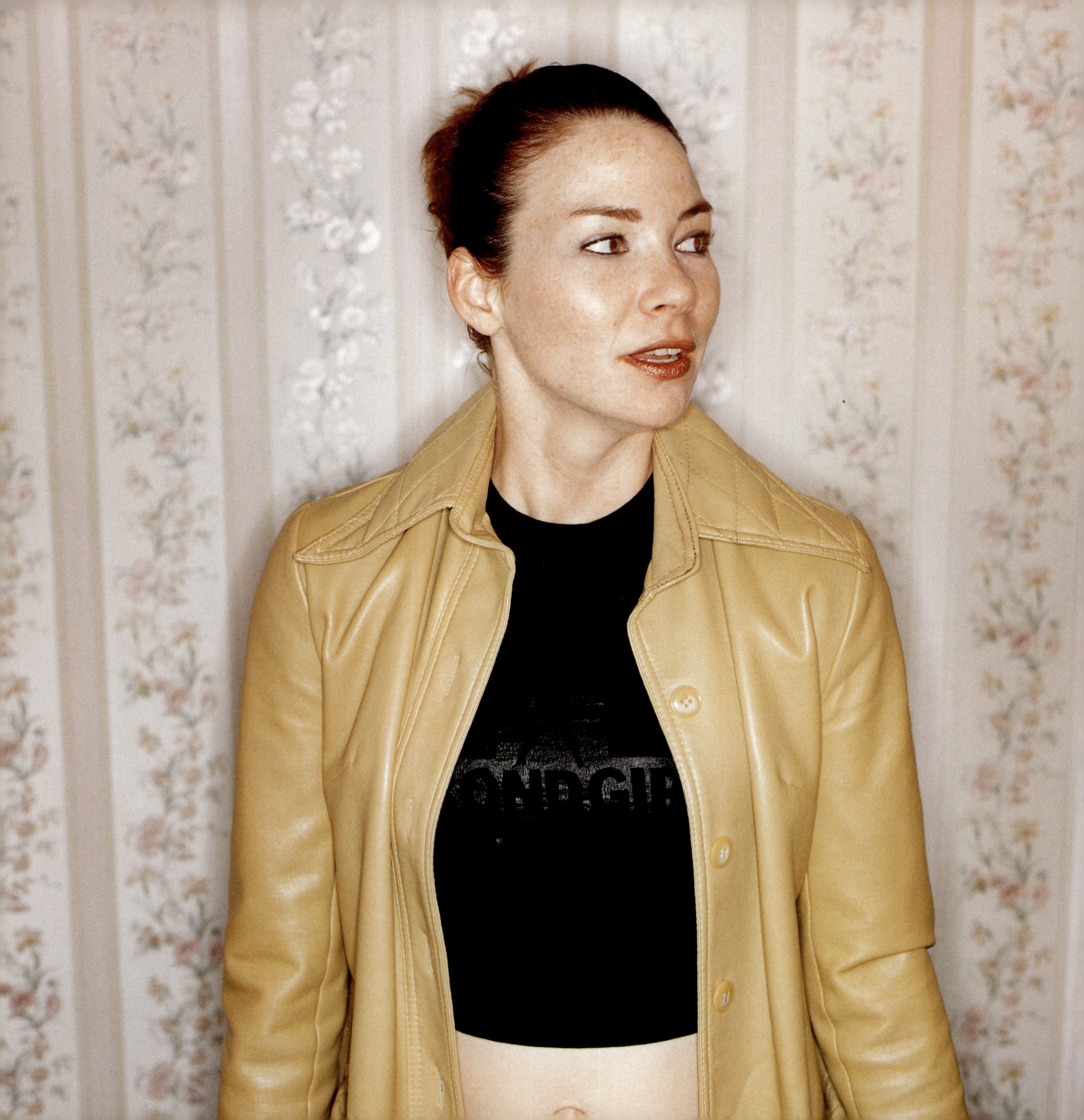

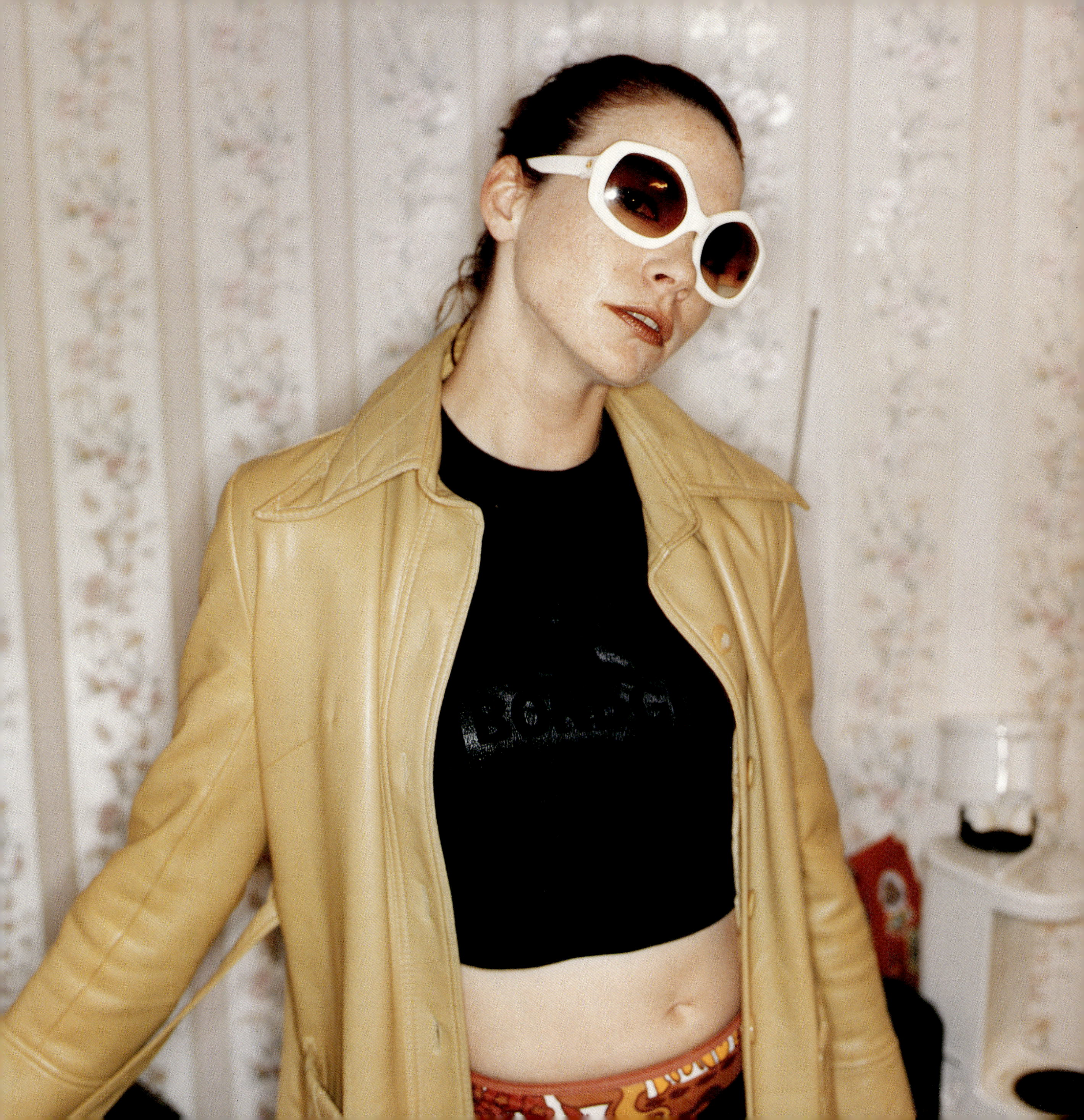

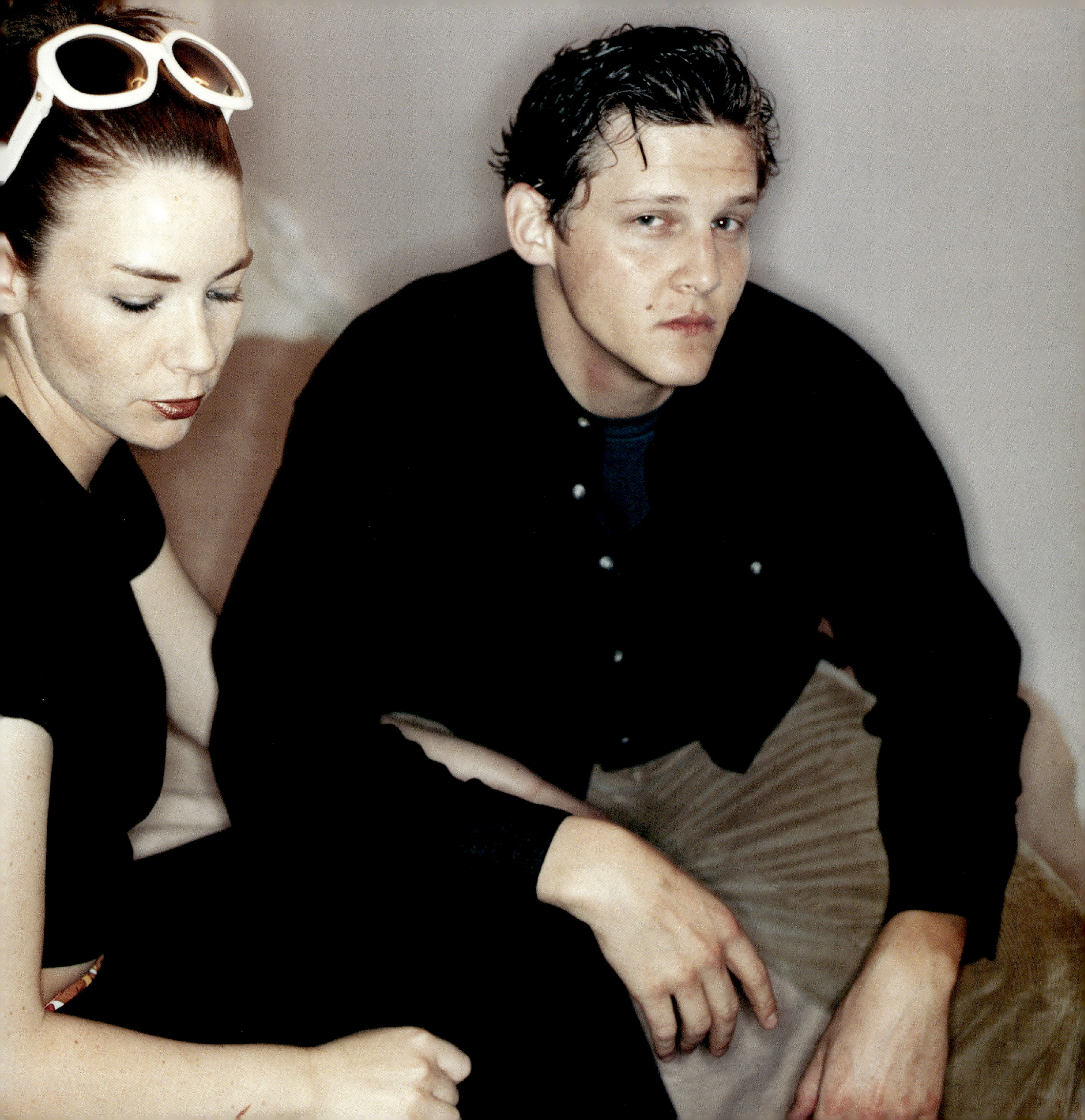

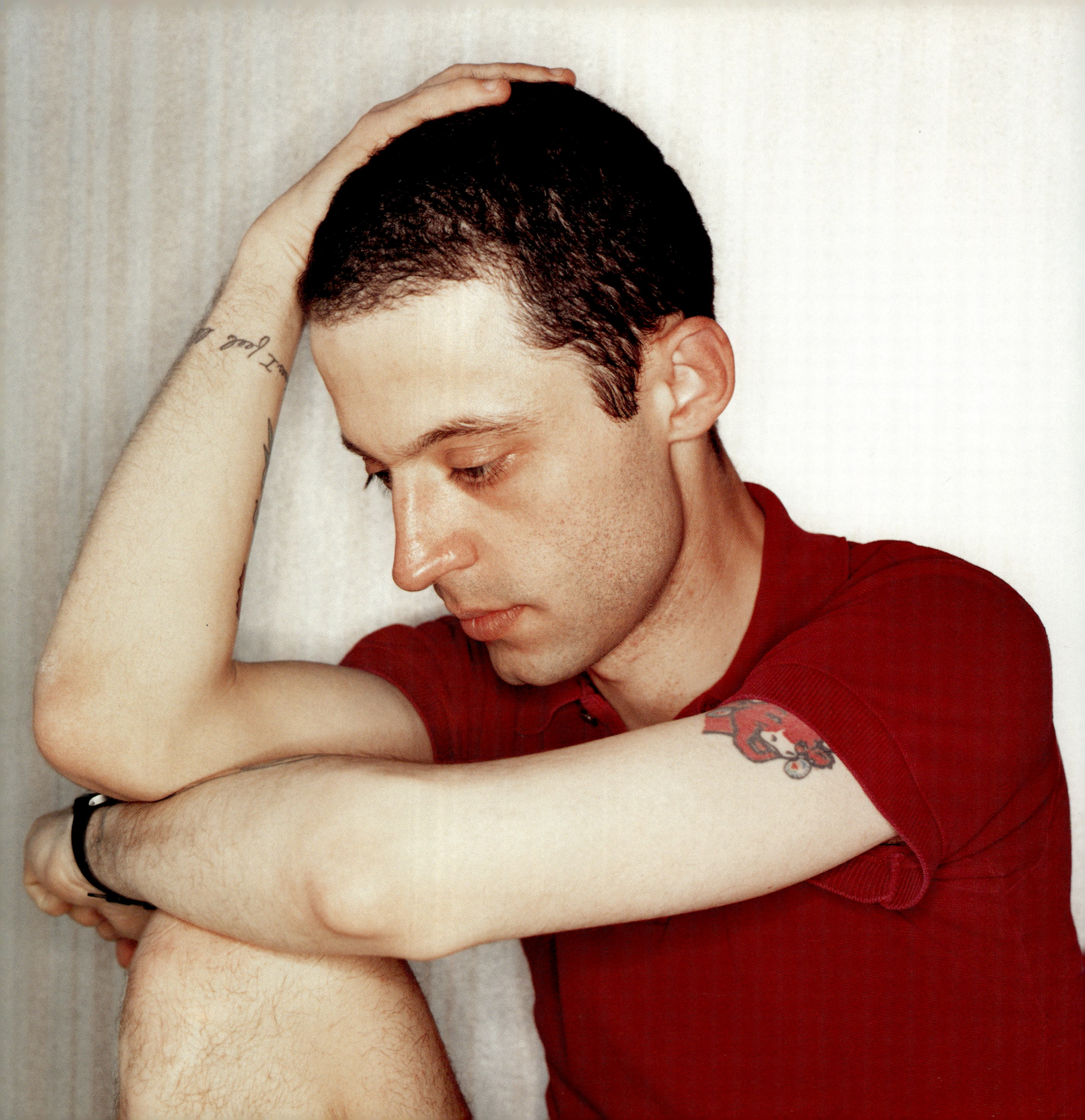

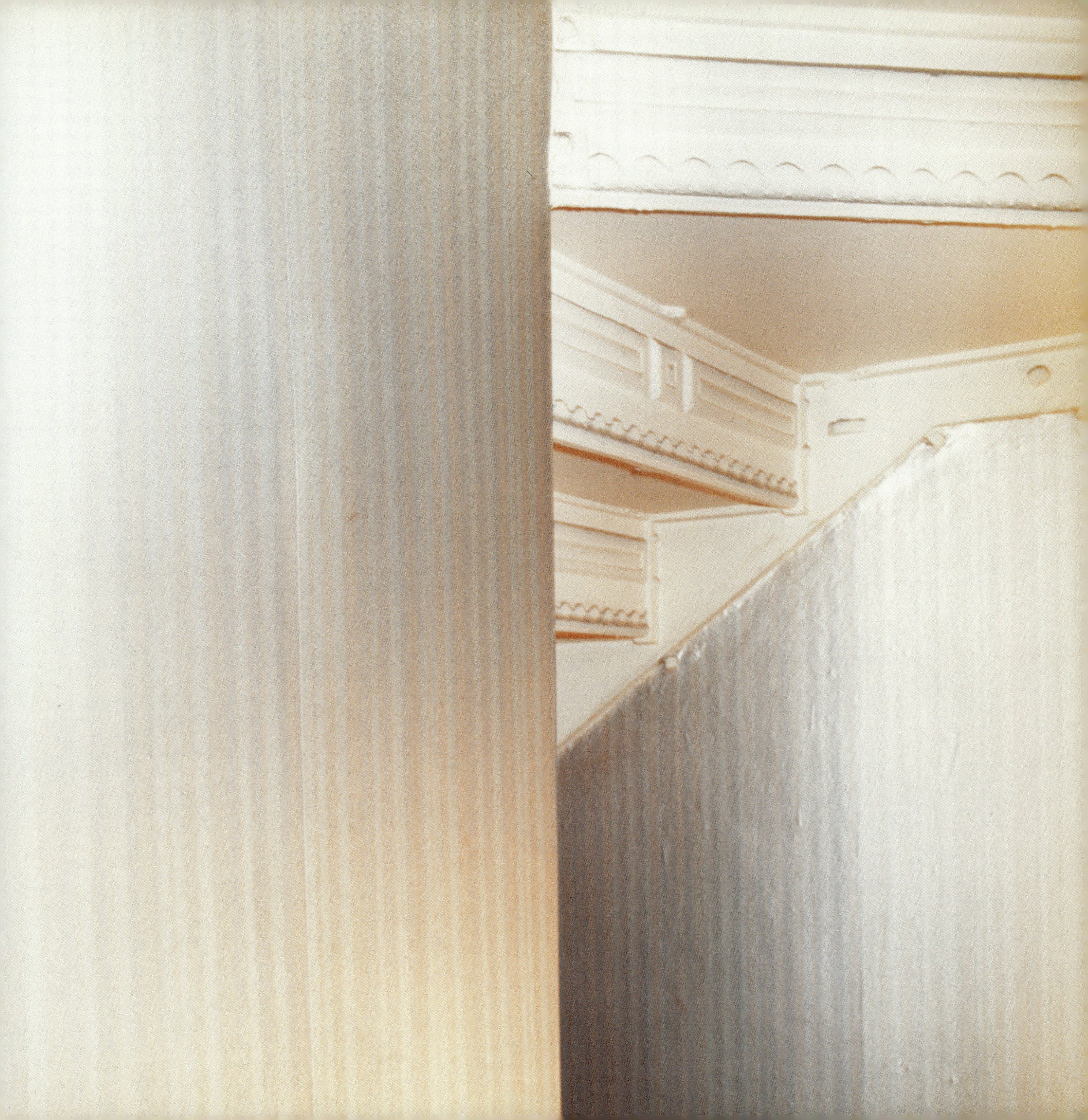

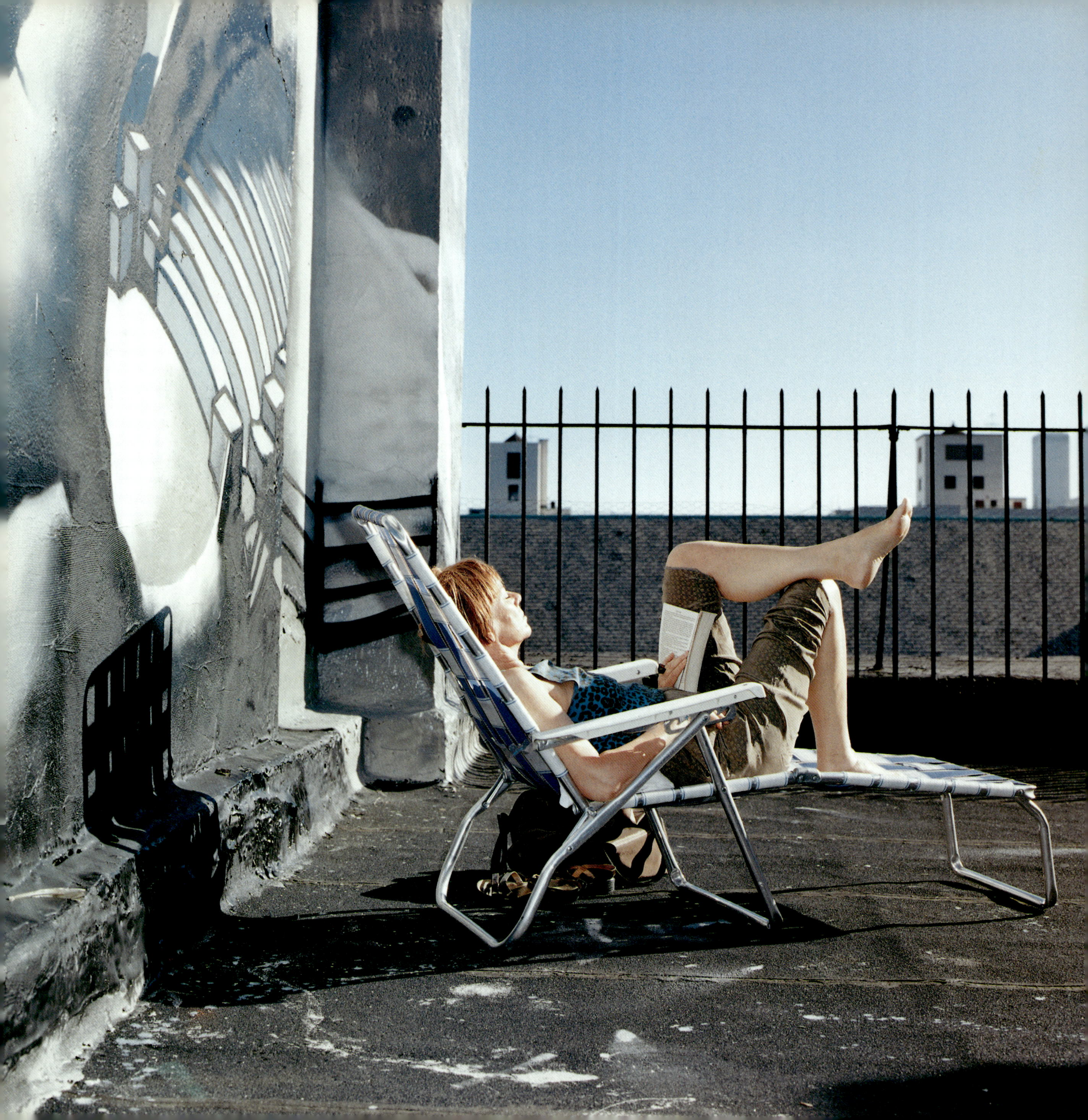

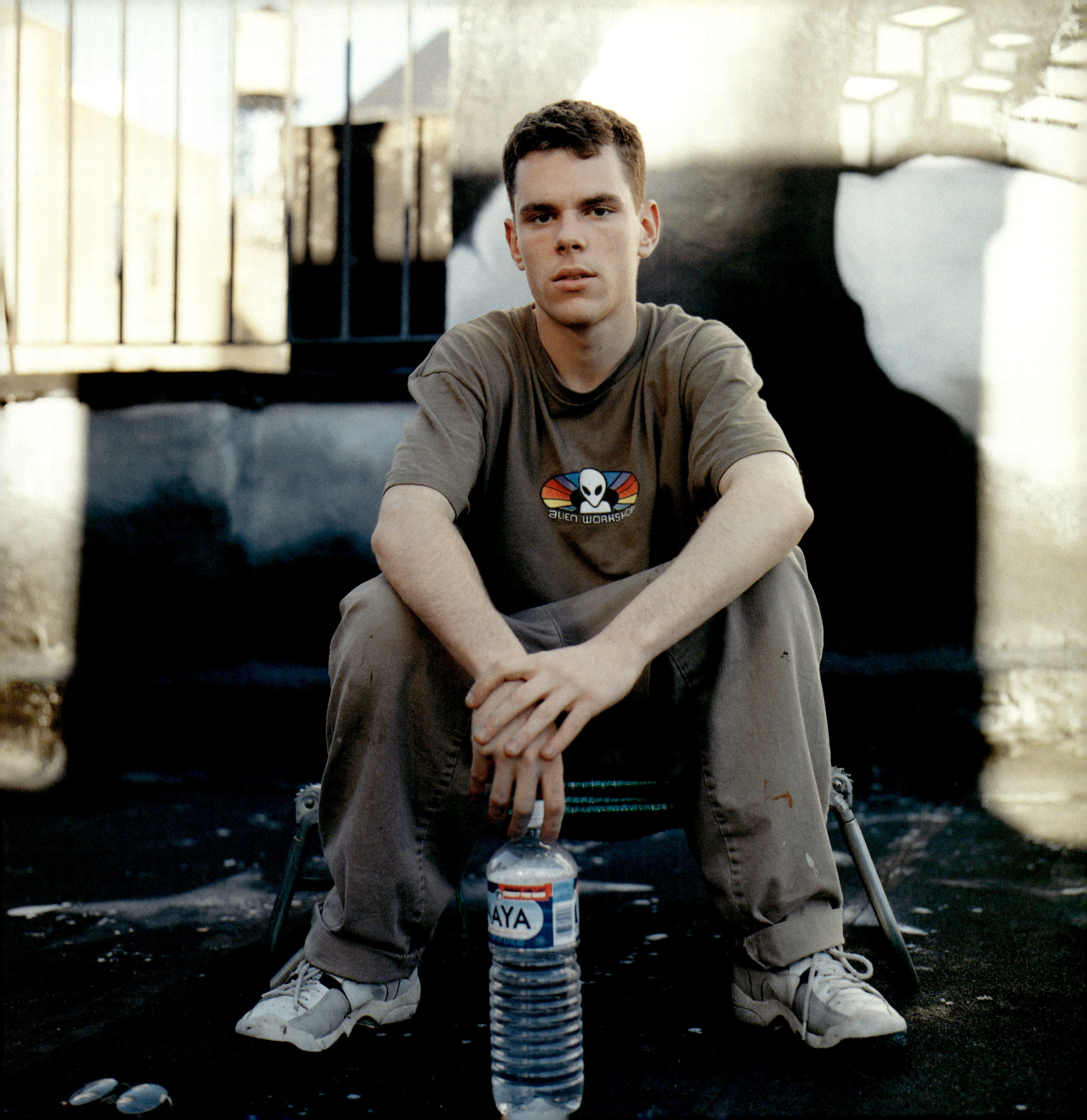
ALIEN WORKSHOP
AYA

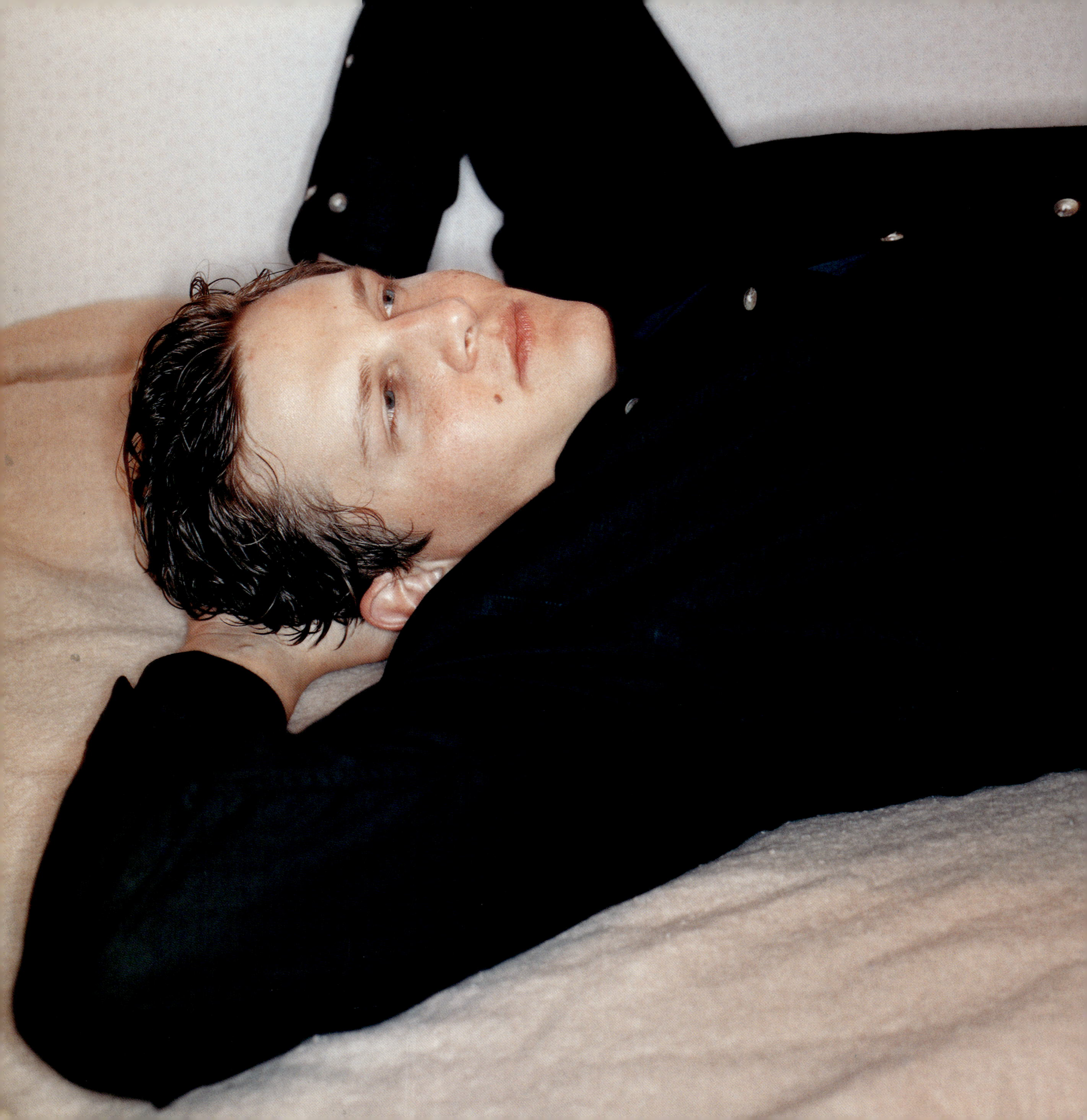

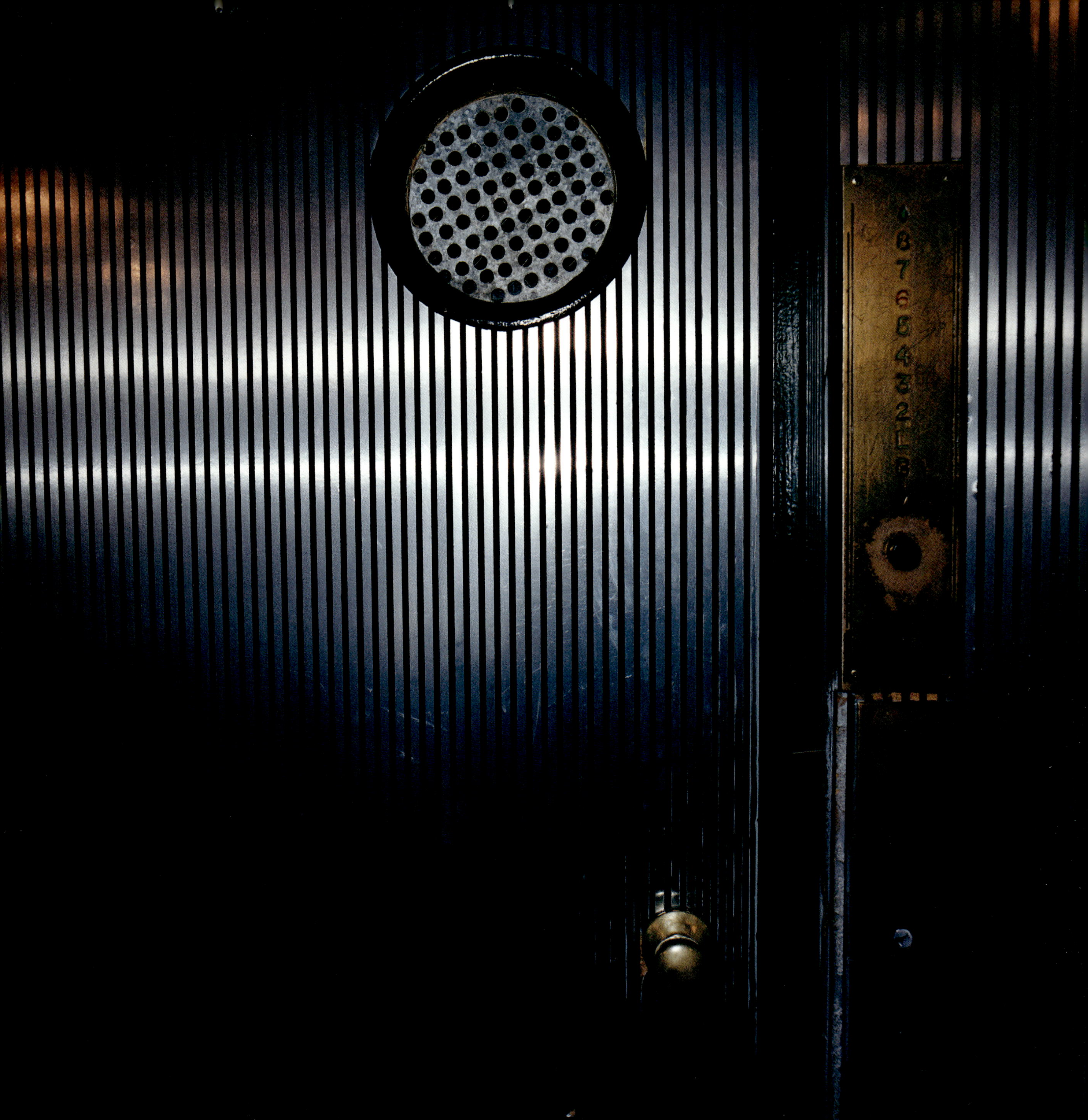
8
7
6
5
4
3
2
L

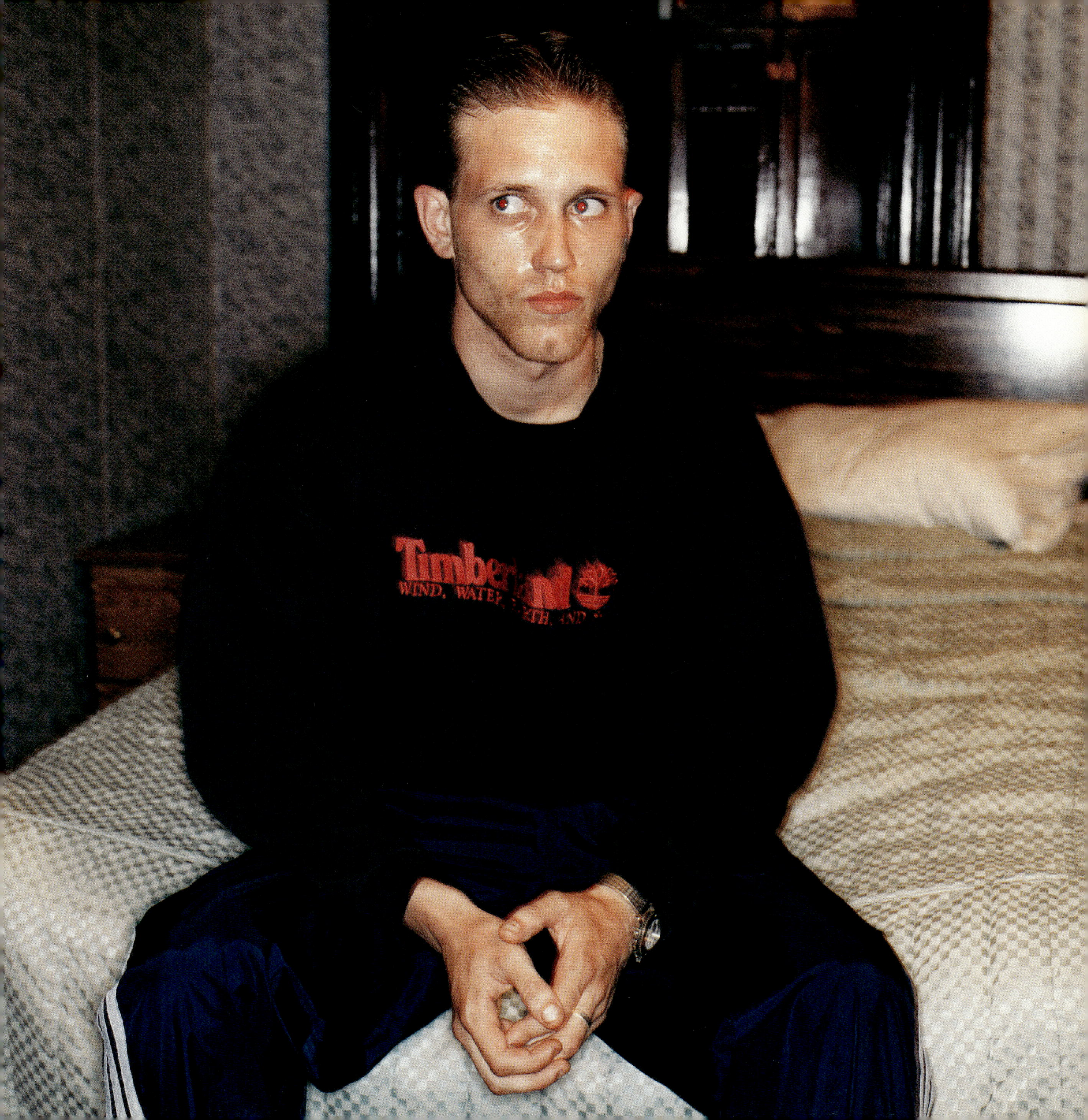
Timberland

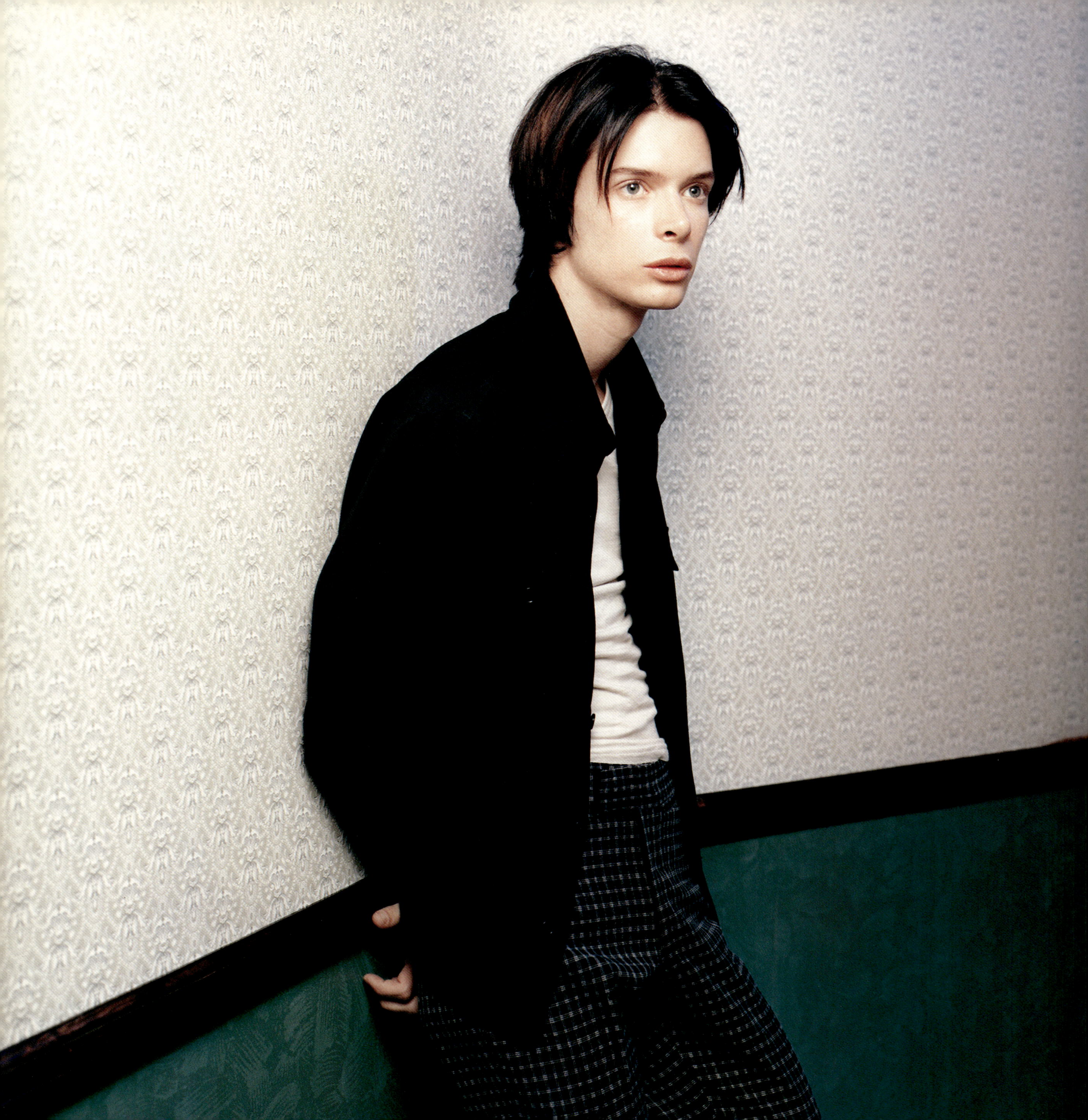

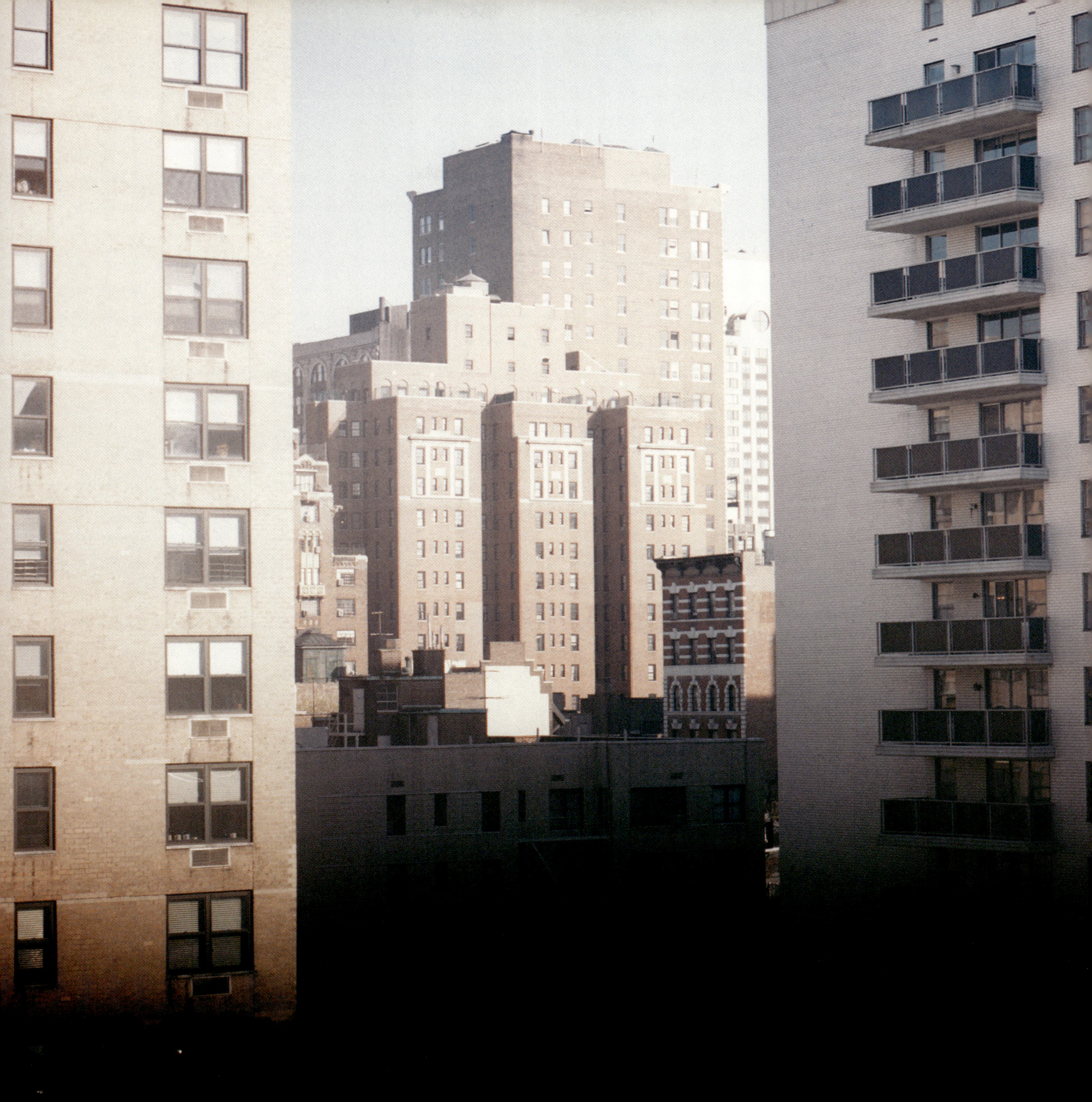

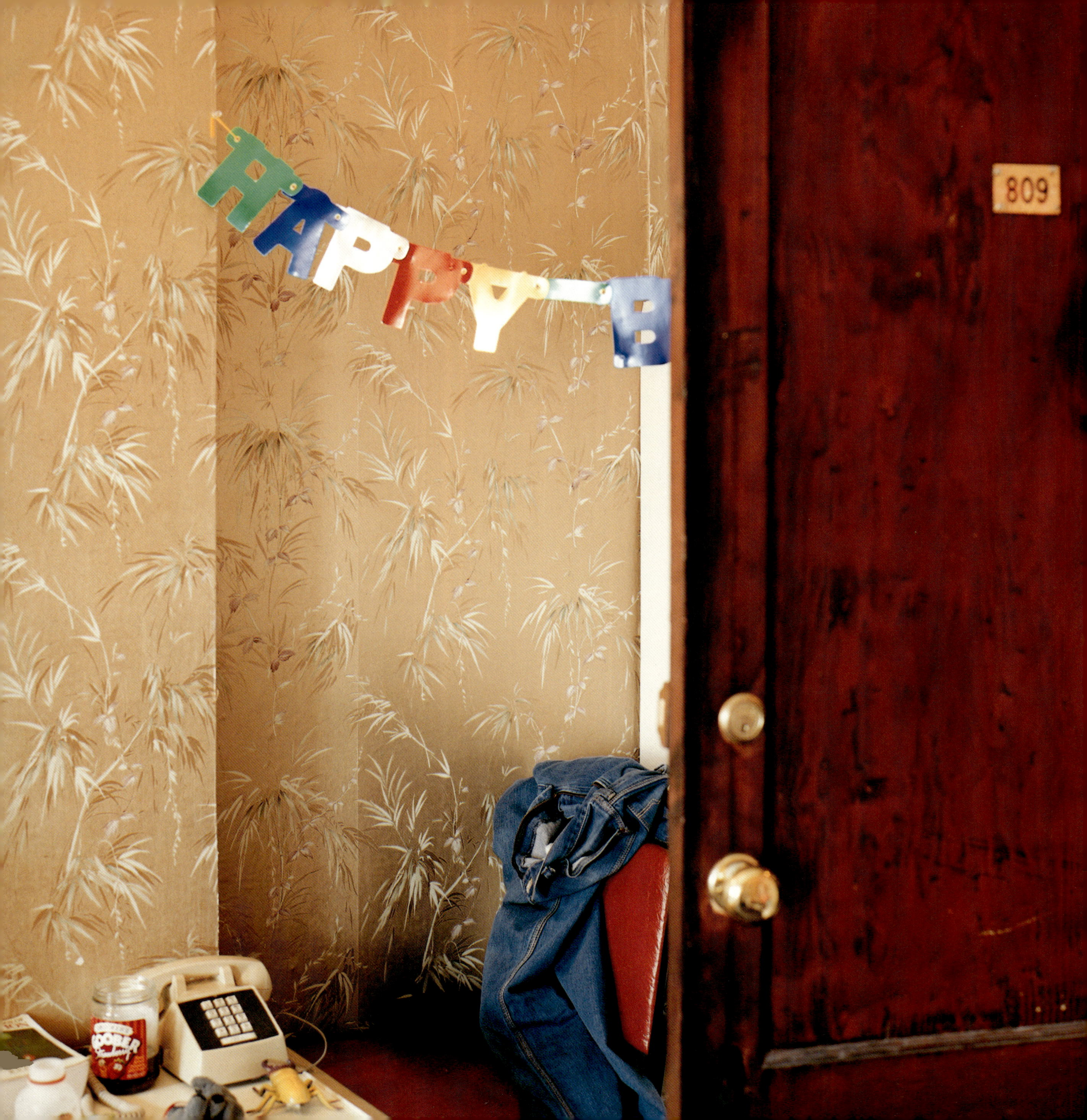
HAPPY B
809

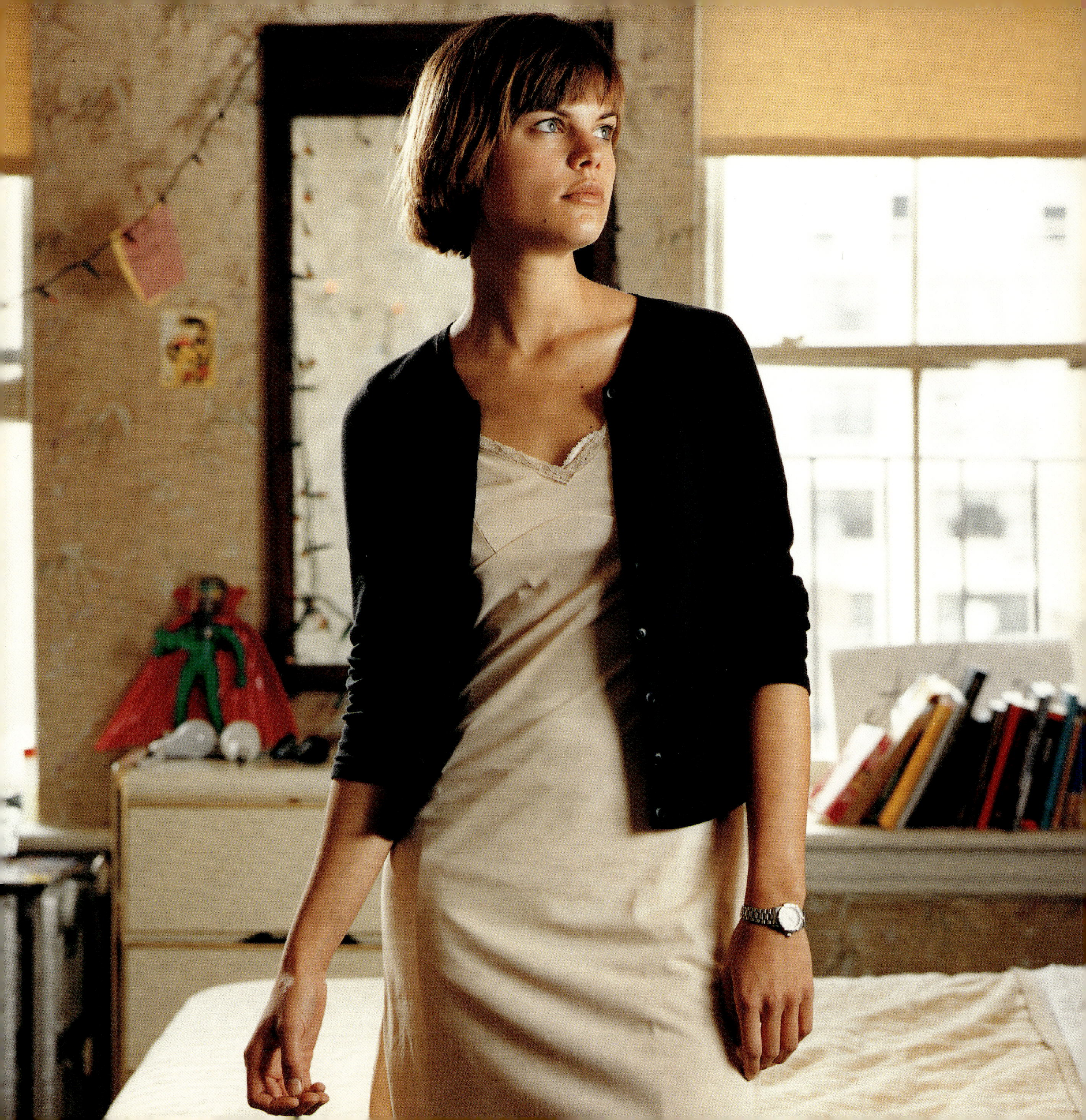

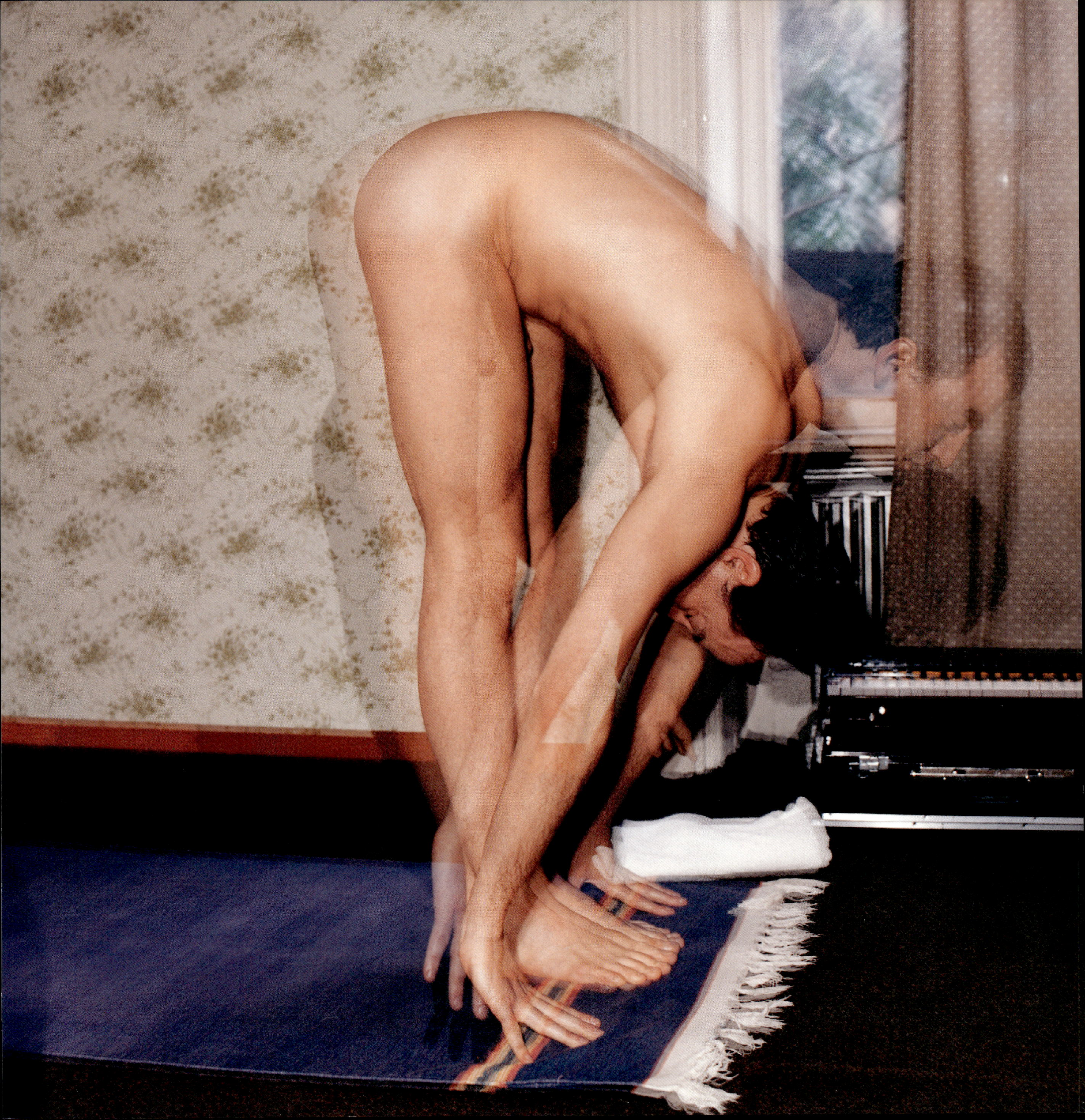

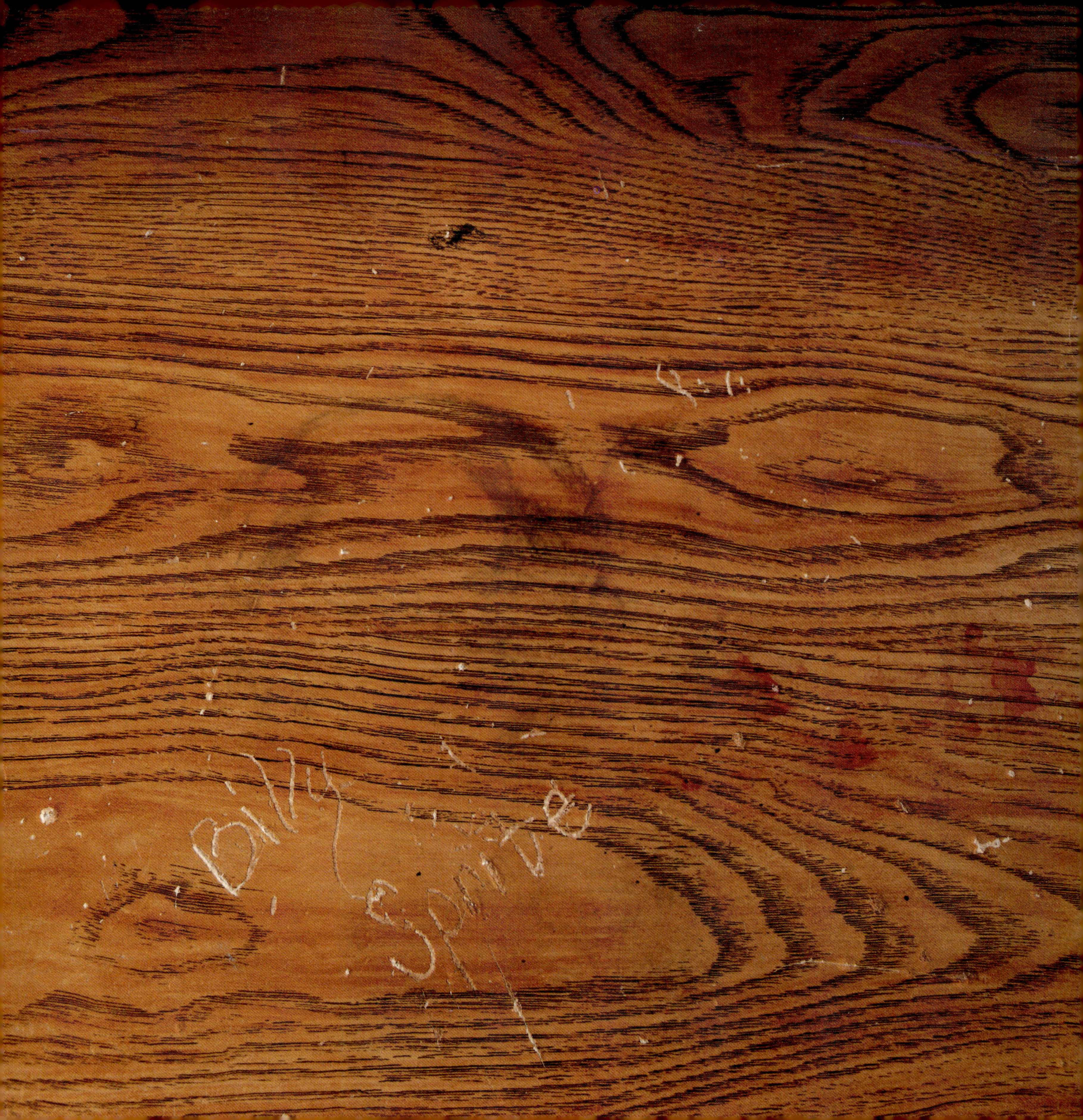
Billy

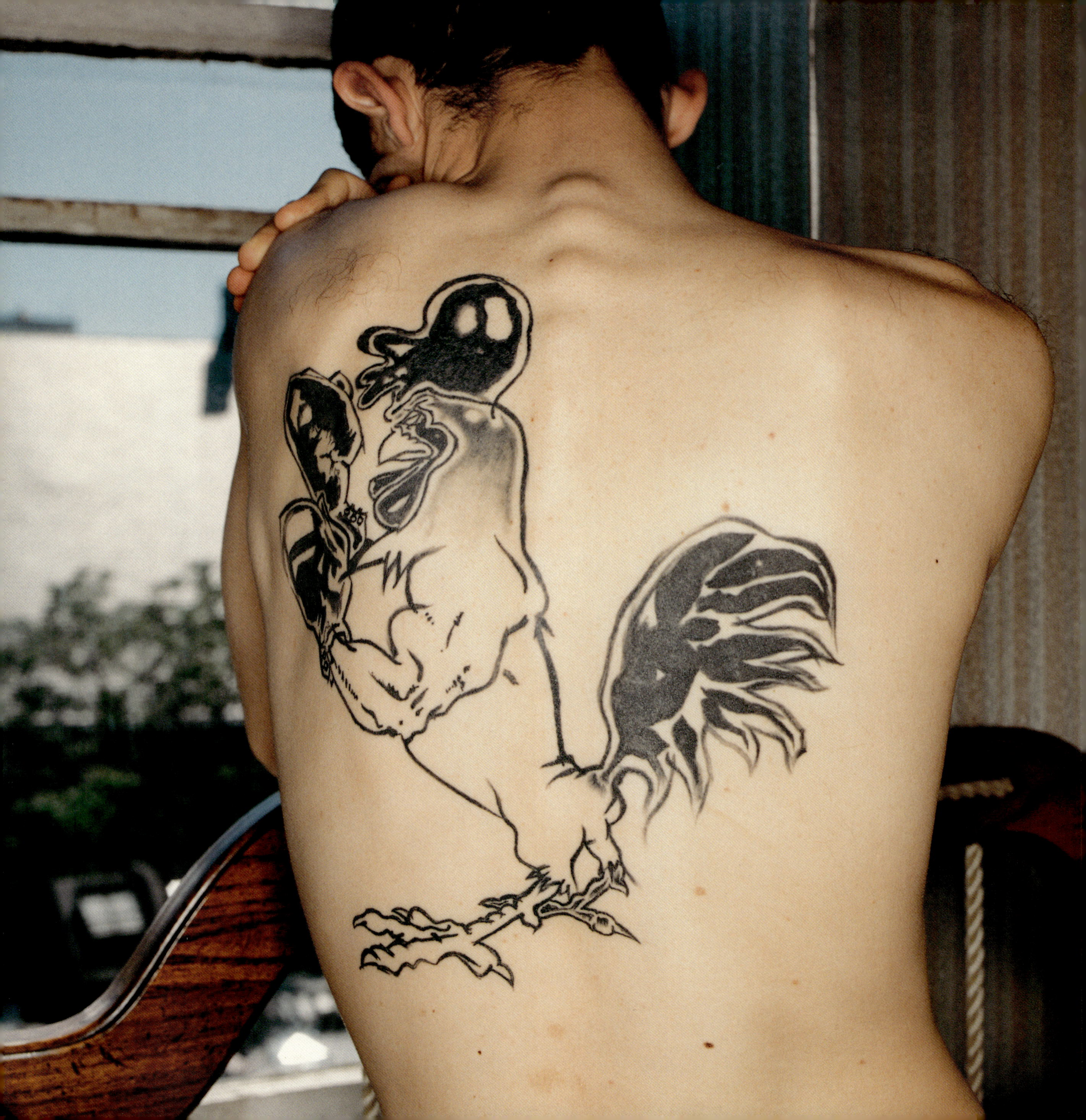

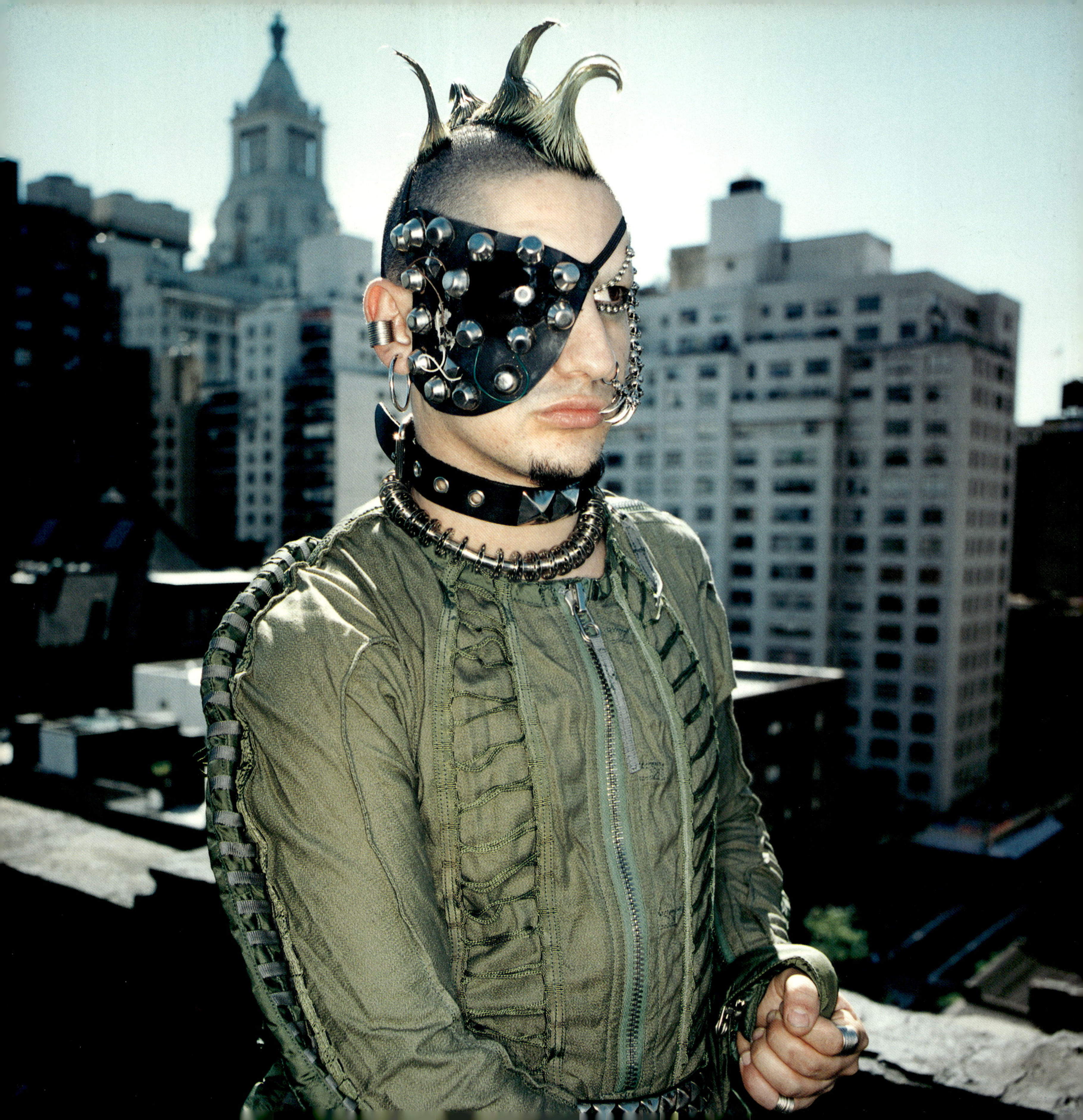

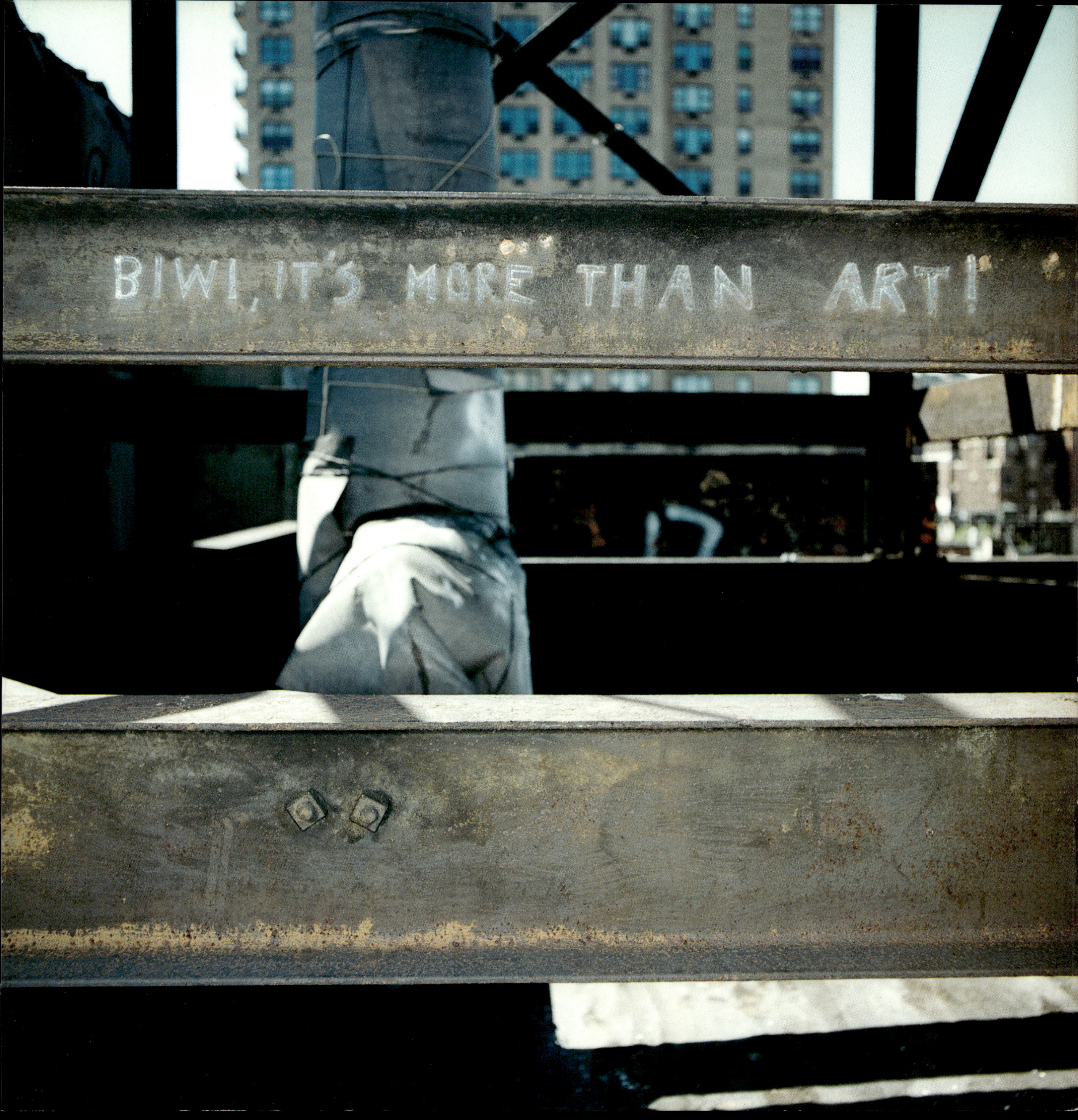
BIWI, IT'S MORE THAN ART!

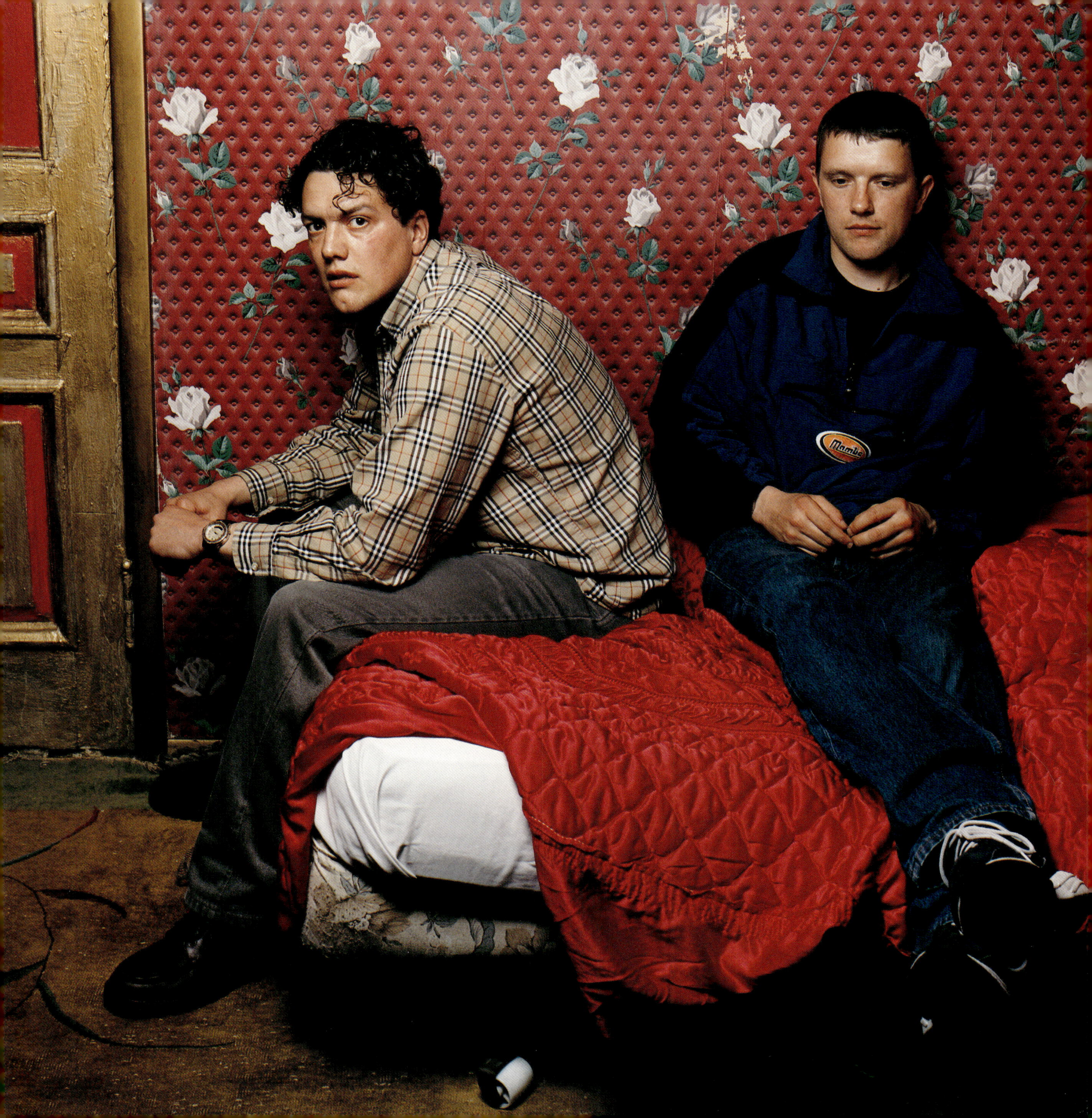
Mambo

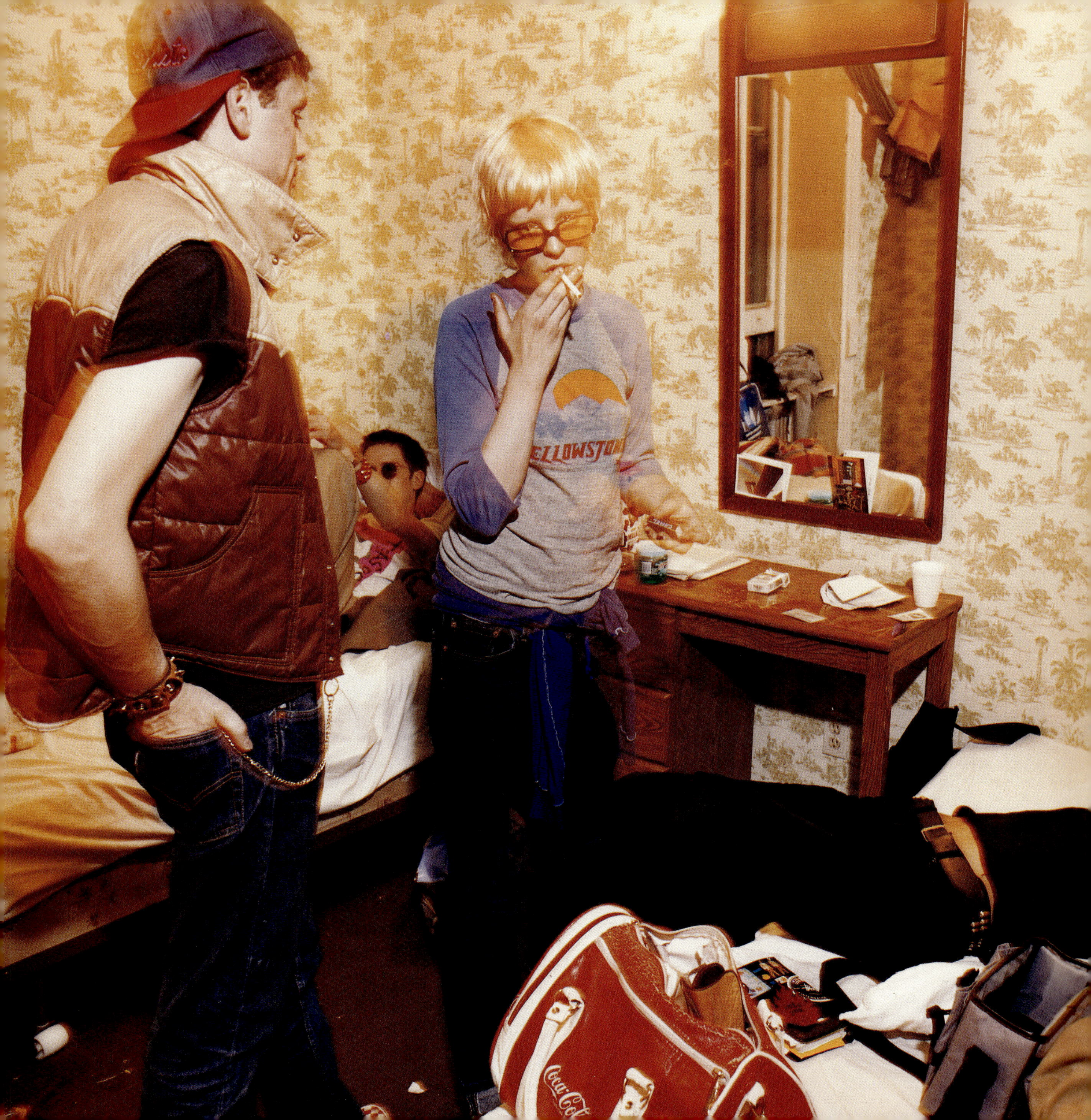

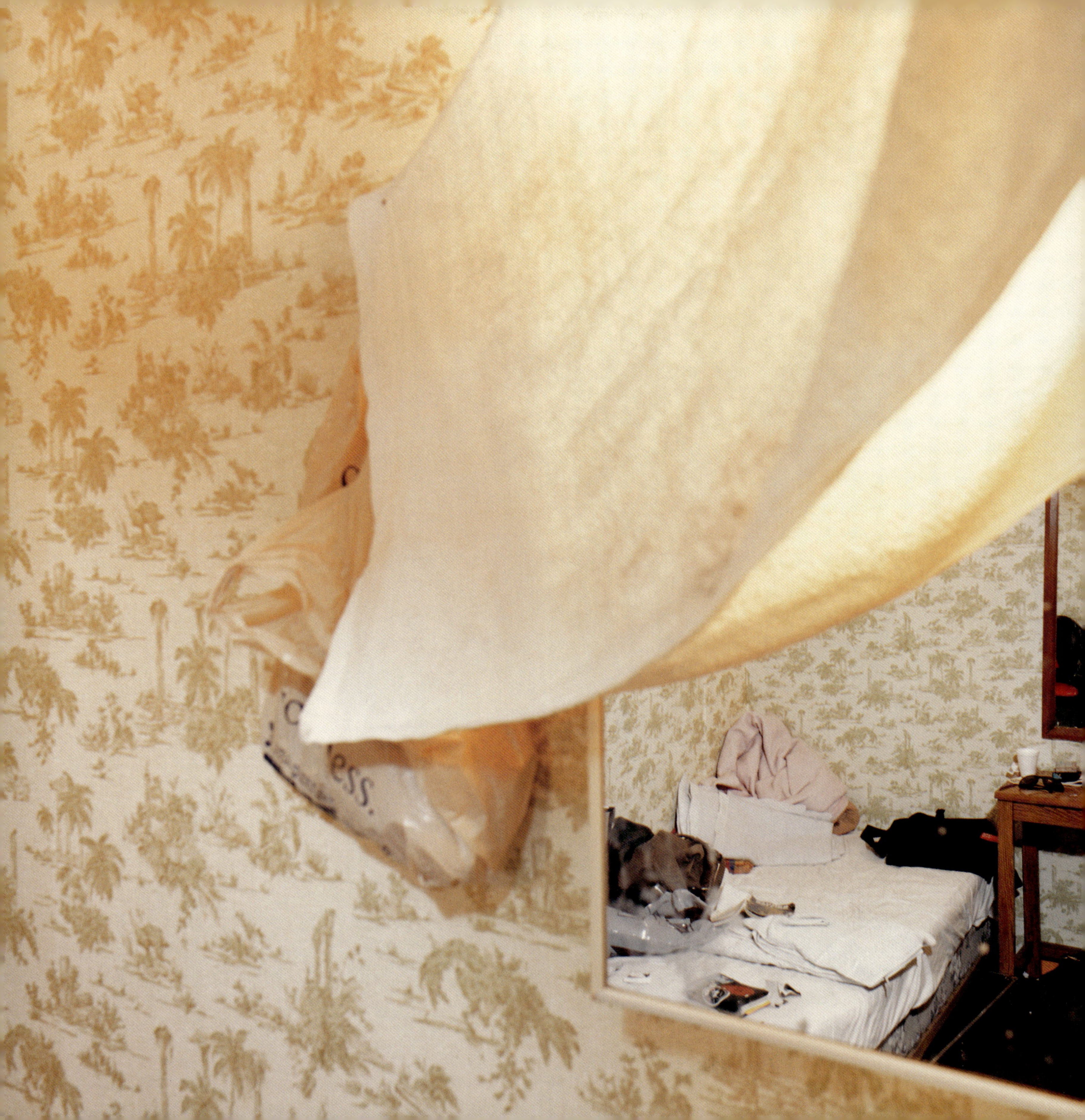

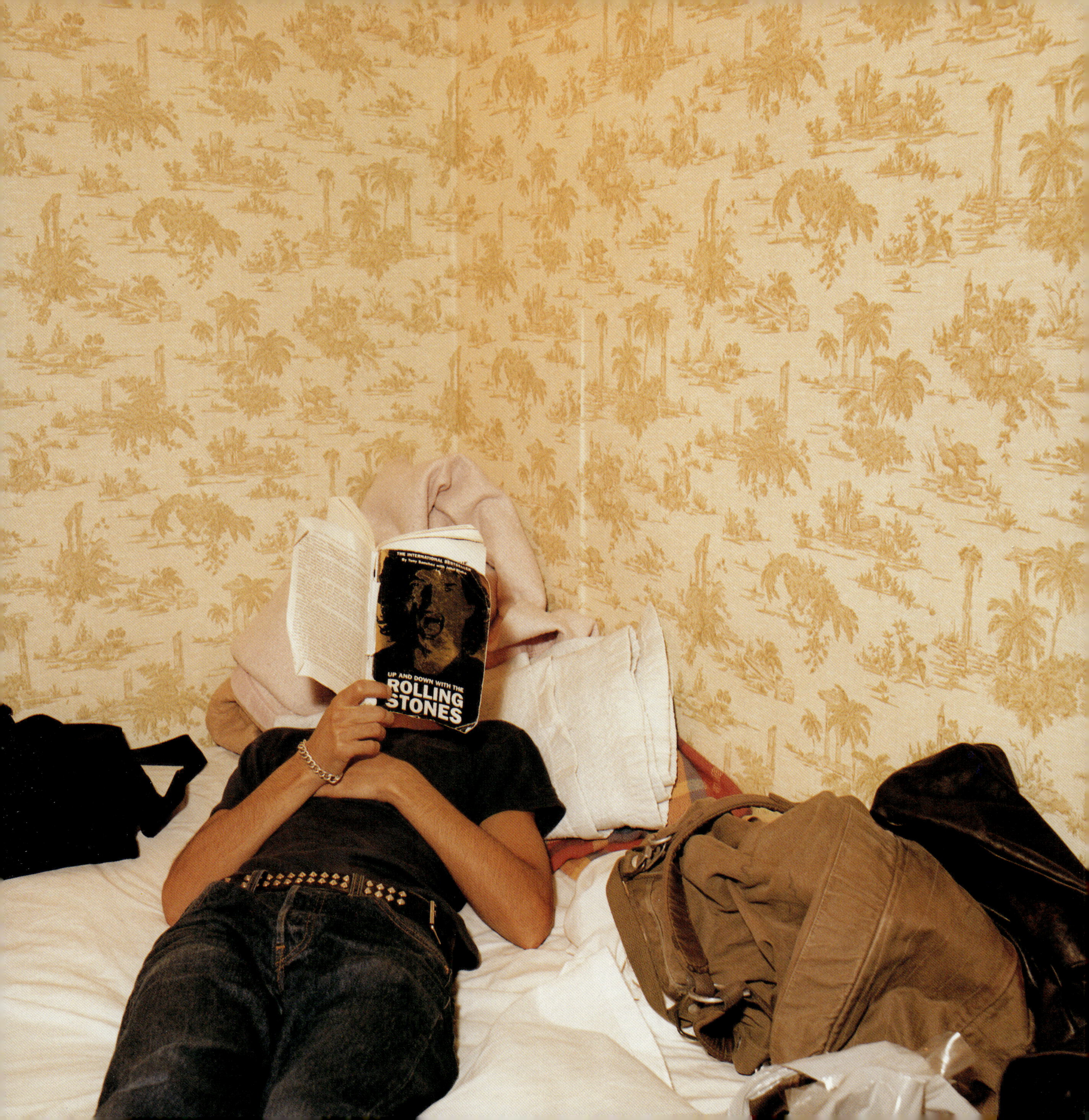
THE INTERNATIONAL BESTSELLER
UP AND DOWN WITH THE
ROLLING
STONES

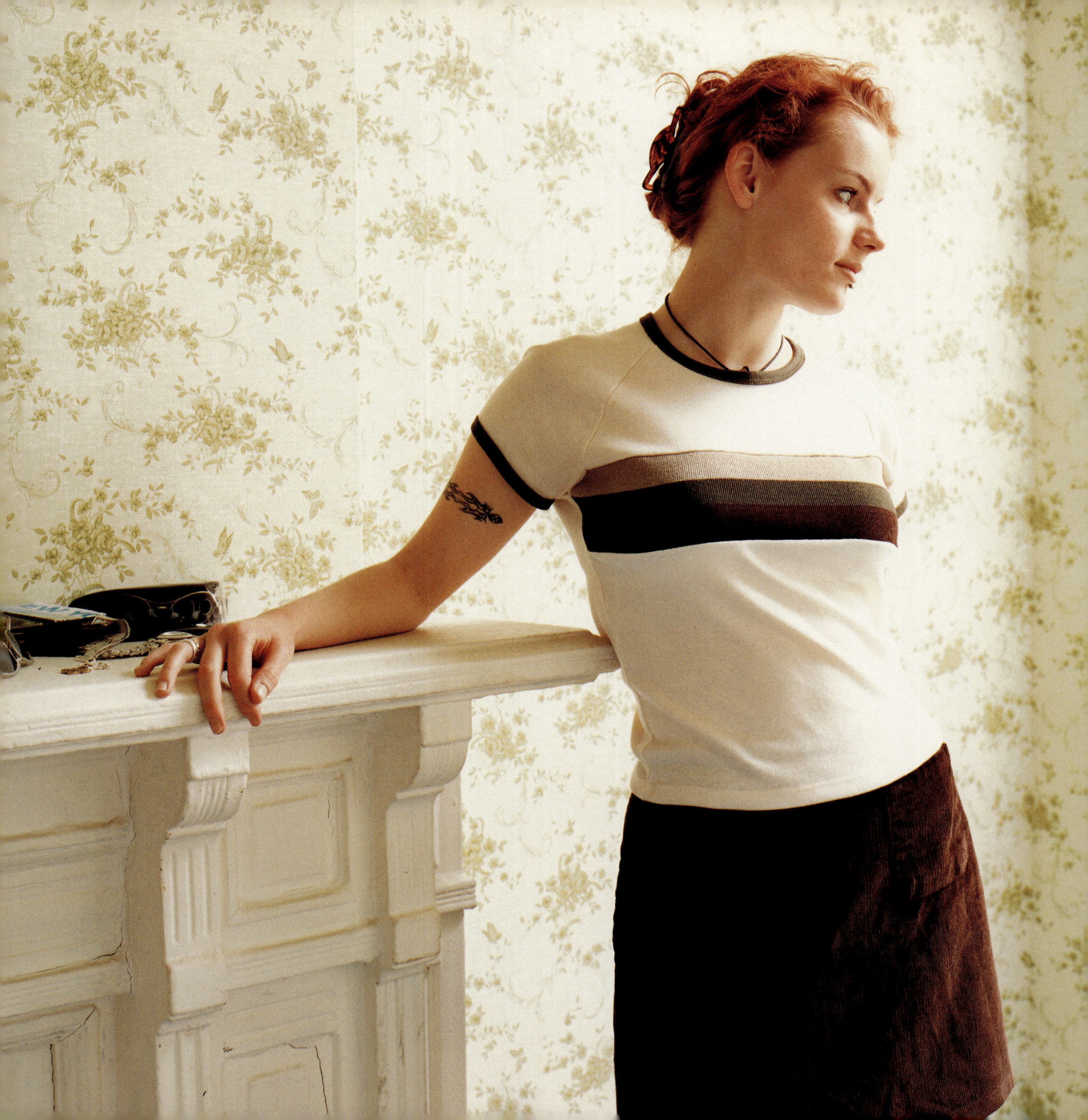

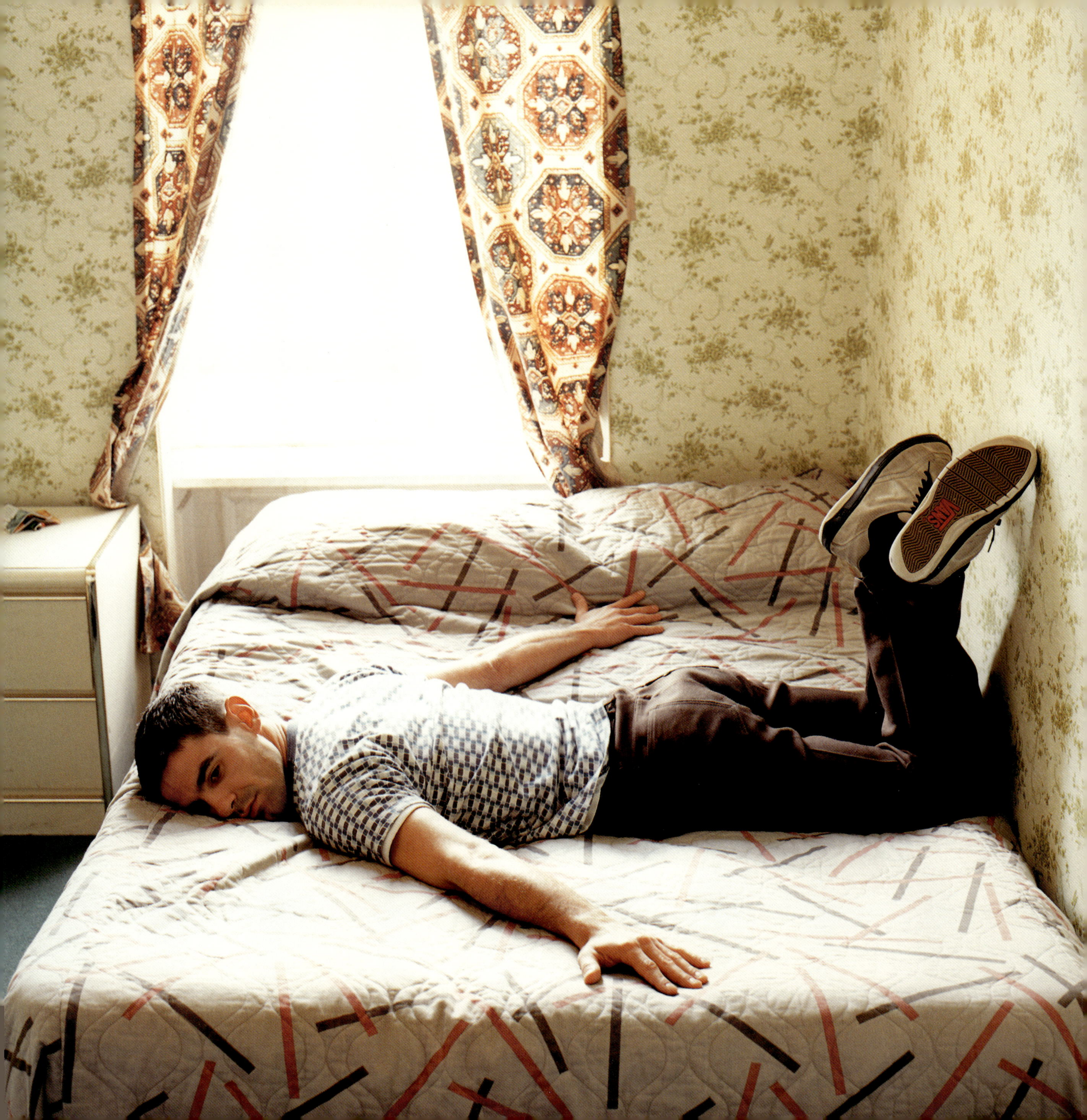
VANS

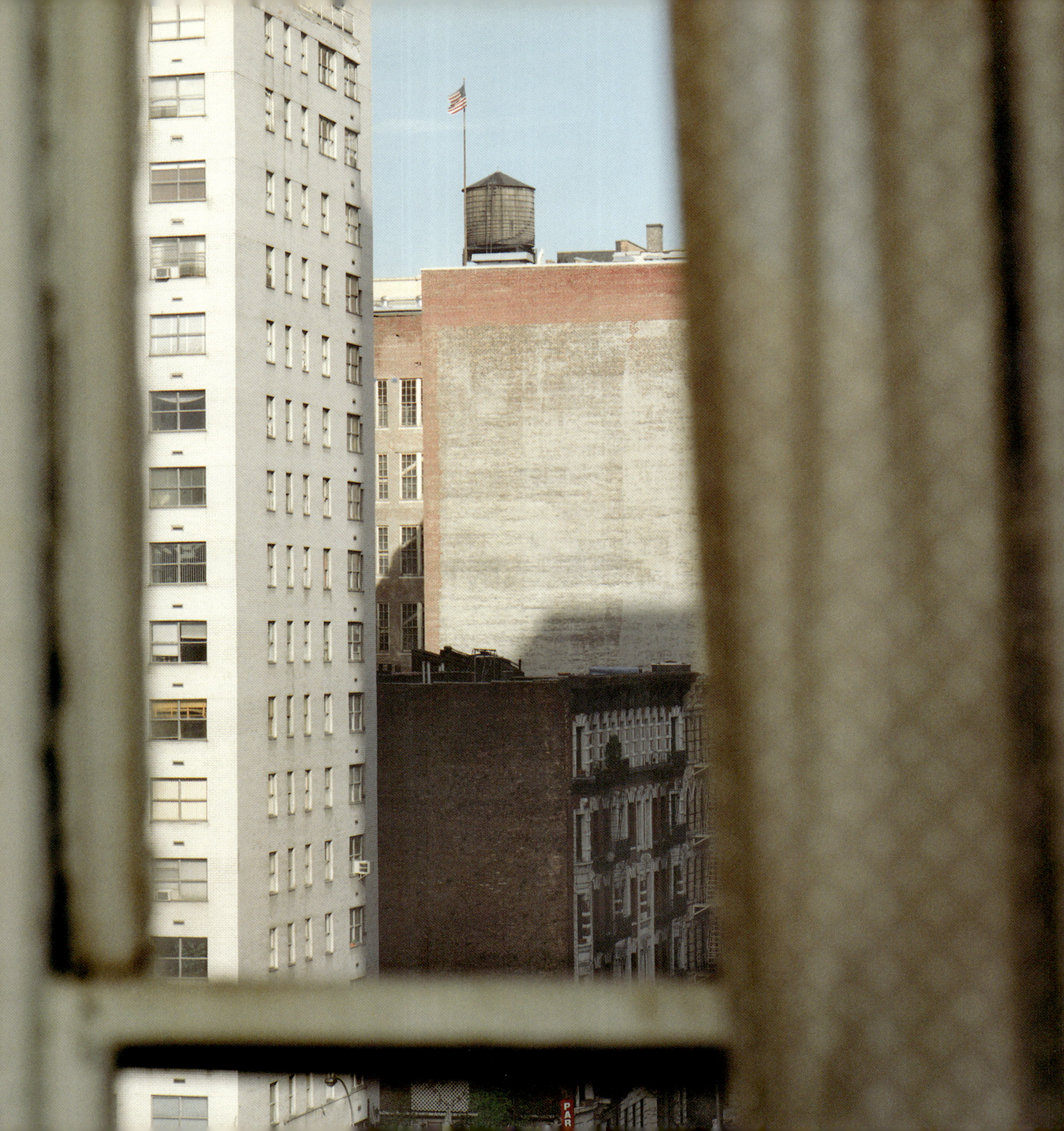
PAR

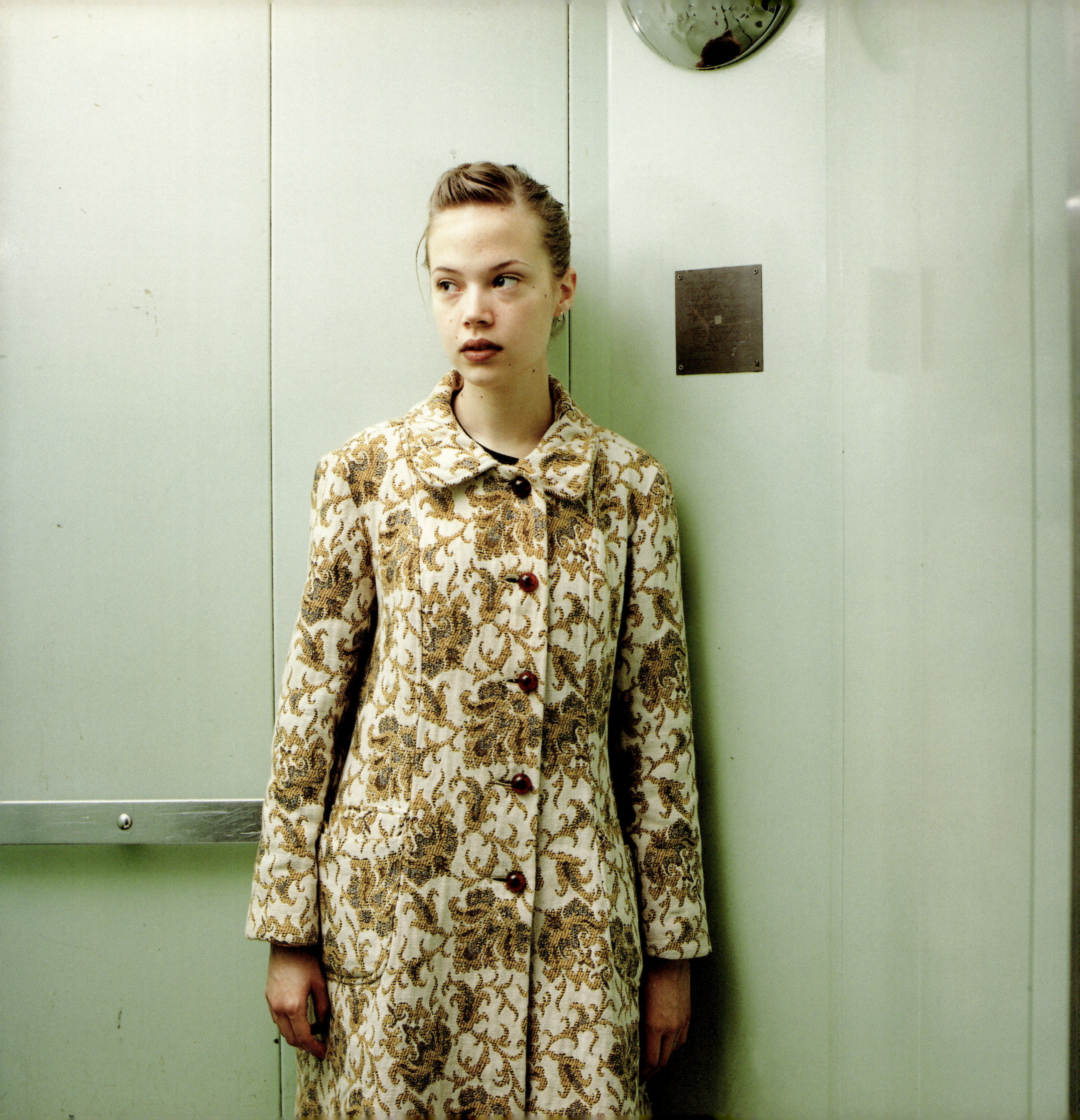

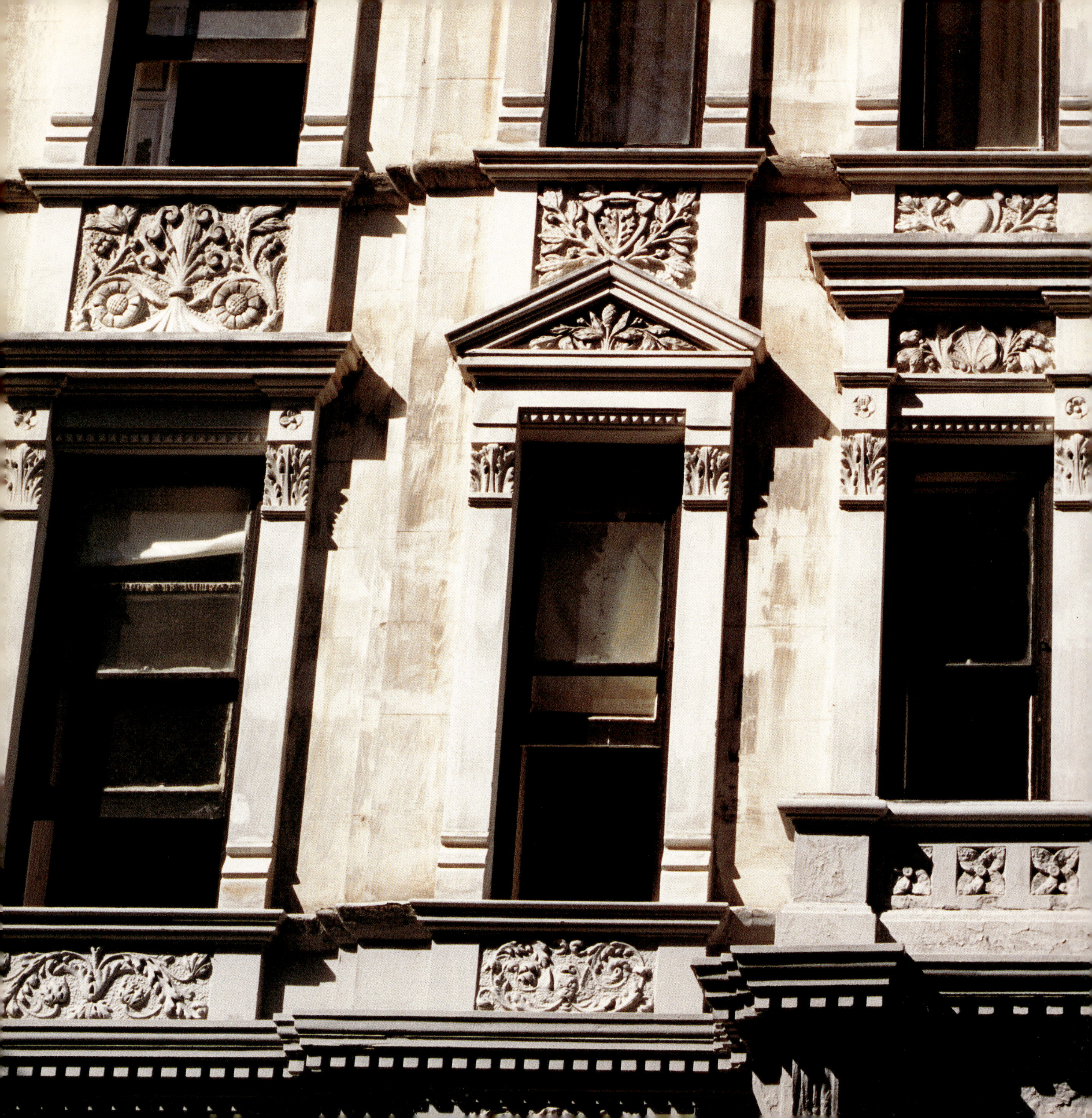

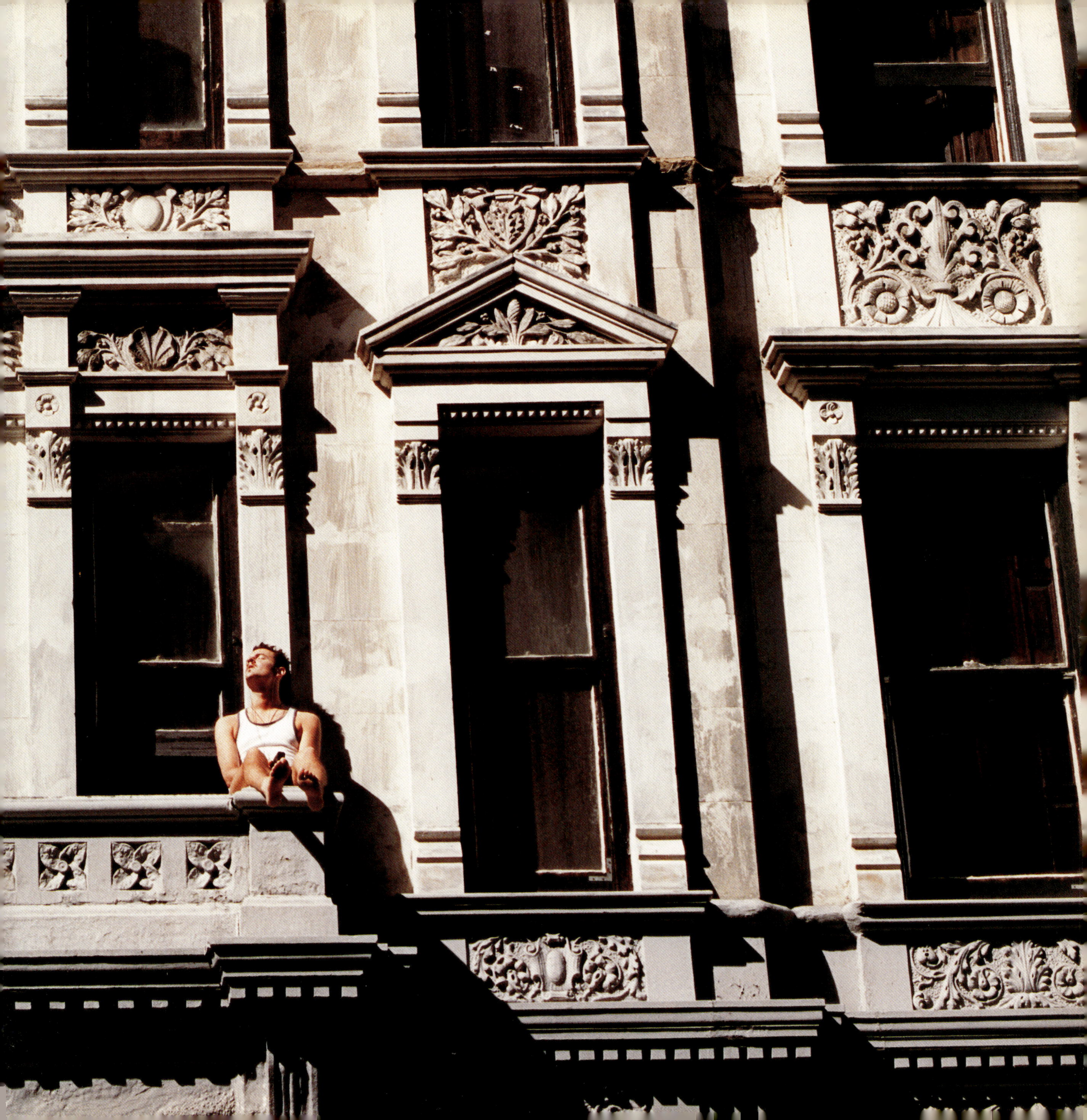